DIALECTICS OF DEFEAT

DIALECTICS OF DEFEAT

THE PROBLEMS OF CULTURE IN POSTCOLONIAL INDIA

G. P. DESHPANDE

Seagull
BOOKS
calcutta 2006

Cover photograph by Naveen Kishore
Cover design by Sunandini Banerjee

ISBN 81 7046 279 7

Published by Naveen Kishore, Seagull Books Private Limited
26 Circus Avenue, Calcutta 700 017, India

Printed in India by Rockwel Offset
55B Mirza Ghalib Street, Calcutta 700 016

For

Janantarasauhridani

(to borrow Kalidasa's famous expression)

of this life and perhaps the next

Contents

Preface

The lectures and essays collected in this volume have been produced over a long period of time. Some of them were written in response to political and cultural developments. I discovered that not all of them were entirely comments on the situations or events here and now. A number of them concerned themselves with the historical experience of the Indian writer and playwright, writing especially in Indian languages. It seems to me that our media and a section of the urban public do not avowedly concern themselves with native cultural expression. Understandably, the problems of our literary culture do not usually get the attention they deserve. A number of writings in this collection address themselves to those problems.

This effort to come to terms with our culture has, of course, been rather sporadic. There is no pretension here to an academic analysis and the approach has been quite eclectic. The reader will find here a magician's bag, as it were. The writing clearly lacks discipline but that has hopefully been compensated for by what I might call radical eclecticism. You will find several things from Buddhism to the Enlightenment project in this writing.

The Indian writer writing in Marathi, Tamil, Bangla or any Indian language stands on a bridge between India and Europe. However, he stands there all alone. European debates have left most of Asia or the erstwhile colonized world far behind. It does not seem as if Algeria or francophone Africa matters to France in any significant way any longer. In that regard, Camus or Lyotard must be the last Algerians or French Algerians. There were never any British Indians in that sense. But there was, at least, an awareness of the mosaic that India happens to be. Now it is a different story. India figures in the English consciousness, if at all, as an undifferentiated ethnic reality. A real India has been replaced by an undifferentiated and therefore an imaginary India. This India is more unreal than Max Mueller's or Monier Williams's India. Normally it would not or should not have mattered. But it does. Because the West decides the parameters of our self-discovery. One need not grudge the status of the West. At least I don't. At the same time it is necessary to see that if our plural and varied cultural memory is not recognized for what it is, we shall have no intellectual or literary strategies to turn this cultural memory into cultural nationalism.

We seem to have two views of India. The West and the West-influenced Indian elite would take the simple way out by accepting the easy formulation of one, undifferentiated India. The Indian nationalist, on the other hand, would advocate another equally undifferentiated India. The difference is that the former approach takes the English-speaking (and largely uncontaminated by the vernacular) Indian and his understanding of India as constitutive of this mythical 'one India'. The other approach consists of an Orientalist understanding of the same. It also—and for that very reason—denies the cultural and literary plurality of India.

This is not a case of amnesia, as more than one analyst has suggested. Rather, it is a manufactured memory that celebrates the non-existent. If one were to look at our media and its coverage of our cultures and literatures, we would notice that, increasingly, it is incapable of handling Indian cultures. The media, therefore, manufactures a cultural reality which pushes the multiplicity of our cultural experience under the rug. It is a simplified reality, indeed two kinds of simplified reality. These essays at one level join issue with that simplified version of (or manufactured) India.

This book is an attempt at working out a dialectic of defeat. The crucial thing is the rupture that the colonial experience brought about in our lives. The present crisis can be understood only in those terms. For, both the versions of India have been the products of that phenomenon. The colonial experience makes modernity and revivalism each other's cousin, in a manner of speaking! These essays are an exploration of that phenomenon. They do not show a way out of our cultural crisis but, hopefully look at that crisis in a clear manner and, in the process, identify some of its features.

There are many friends who encouraged me to write these essays who are too numerous to mention here. They naturally do not agree with all my prognostications. But they have been kind enough to keep me in this business, forever encouraging me to take the kind of positions that I have. Almost every one of these essays has been written because some friend or the other insisted that I must. I can only hope that in this collected form these essays read well and—more importantly—make a point.

G. P. DESHPANDE

The Indian Artist and the 'Long Revolution'

> The moment the arts and commerce penetrate into the lives of the 'people' and create new means of riches, which gives strength to the labour class, it prepares itself for the revolution.
>
> —Barnave, *Introduction à la Revolution Française,* written in 1792, published in 1834[1]

1

There has always been an image of Indian arts and crafts which is not so much unreal as it is a motivated structuring of the Indian reality. This image,. an extension of the notions of 'Orientalism' developed by colonizing Europe, also came to to be shared by the Indian elite over the nearly two hundred and fifty years of contact with the colonizing West. In this image, the arts were looked upon as a form of shining mystique; inexplicable and immutable art forms that had to be and were received with rapturous welcome. It was the same with Indian philosophy. The ideals of the Upanishads needed and have always got an European interpreter in every century since the eighteenth. Yeats's enthusiasm for Rabindranath Tagore's philosophy-poetry was but one example of how Indian arts and spiritualism have been a part of the Western search for the Oriental spirit—for those indescribable art forms and structures which are, strictly speaking, beyond modern aesthetics. Indian art provided yet another evidence of the correctness of the 'ontological and epistemological' distinction between the 'Orient' and the 'Occident'.[2] It was true of literature, it was true of philosophy, it was true also of music. How does one explain otherwise the 'melodic arts', so to speak, beginning in Japan and ending up somewhere on the eastern and southern shores of the Mediterranean? The Orient was mystical. It was good and right that it was so.

The Indian elite, particularly since Independence, has swallowed the 'mystique of the Orient' theory. Throughout the past few decades, a strange revivalism has been in operation; a revialism which has ignored the sense of imperial superiority inherent in the Orientalist view. Eliot once said of Henry James that 'he had a mind so fine that no idea could violate it'. The Oriental mystique draws its strength precisely from such an assumption. No modern idea can violate the mystique of the Orient—modern-day Indian revivalism in the arts has based itself upon this premise. If there is a crisis in literary theory, go back to *kavyaprakasha* or *kavyadarsha.* If theatre has failed to give you what it should, go back to the *Natyashastra* and find out where the musicians should sit on the stage, what kind of *yavanika* should be used, what kind of dances are recommended, and when, and so on. Imperialism used its Orientalist scholarship (that individual Orientalists might have been and indeed were fascinated by Asian societies and arts was, of course, true) essentially to emphasize the uniqueness of the Oriental world and thereby to dominate it. Lord Balfour, defending the British supremacy in Egypt, said:

> I take no attitude of superiority. But I ask [Robertson or anyone else] . . . who has even the most superficial knowledge of history, if they will look in the face the facts with which a British statesman had to deal when he is put in a position of supremacy over the great races like the inhabitants of Egypt . . . Look at all the oriental countries. Do not talk about superiority or inferiority.[3]

'Just rule them', is what Lord Balfour is saying. 'Yes, the Orient is great, let us rule it and make it greater' is his message.

It is important to remind ourselves of these origins of Orientalism because the post-Independence 'revivalism' I am referring to has become a major tendency in Indian writing on arts and literature. To borrow an expression from Walter Benjamin, this 'overtaking of the productive passion' in the name of pure Indianism will reach its sterile limits sooner or later.

With the beginning of the seventies, however, there has been considerable activity in the Indian arts which has moved away from this Orientalist perspective. In our literatures (India has many literatures; to talk of an Indian literature is no more meaningful than to talk of an European literature) there has developed an increasing impatience with the revivalist view. Given the Indian situation, this view entailed the dominance of literature by the higher castes and classes. Purely in terms of the social origins of our writers, the emphasis has now clearly shifted. The dominance of the *bhadralok* (gentry) in the creative enterprise has not altogether disappeared (it cannot and need not), but the number of writers from the lower castes and classes has shot up phenomenally. The various Dalit and revolutionary writers' movements in different parts of India speak of the changed and rapidly changing literary scene in the country. This shift has signalled, on such a wide scale for the first time, two things: one, the traditional notions of who deals in the written word have changed and are changing; and second, the new writer may not be interested in recreating the great Indian spirit typified by our 'great' works, beginning with the Vedas and the Upanishads. These works, they will readily concede, are great but not quite relevant to their existence or to their struggles today. The 'Oriental' wisdom is, in short, no longer the source of Indian creativity, i.e. the creativity that is dominating the Indian scene today. The tradition is being used but in a critical spirit and in much the same way as an artist anywhere in the world would. The Oriental-Occidental divide does not seem meaningful to the contemporary Indian writer or artist. It does not tell him anything about his creativity or his problems. The so-called Oriental or Indian attitude to art is not and cannot be a theoretical construct. It is like understanding Goethe or Schiller in terms of Germanism or Occidentalism. What the artist needs today is a critical aesthetic theory; all the romanticism going with a typical Oriental or Indian *Weltanschauung* cannot provide that to him.

2

The Indian search for a critical aesthetic theory has become significant in the context of the artist's increasing awareness of the divided world in his life; this world is no longer a single, unified, harmonious one. In the days of the nationalist movement it was still possible and even necessary to think of our world of experience as one whole reality which could be interpreted differently. It has not been appreciated fully that the social reality which made for this homogeneity was itself a product of an anti-imperialist movement and, as such, was not an immutable, eternal reality. The thirty-seven years of independent India have, if anything, contributed to an increased awareness of our fragmented world. The 'common culture' in the sense in which Raymond Williams would use the term or in the sense in which F. R. Leavis would view culture, is simply not there.[4] We have, instead, fragments.

The most remarkable fact of the cultural experience of the various peoples of post-Independence India has been this fragmentation of which, naturally, there have been differing and, at times, contradictory interpretations. Some have seen it in the Indian artist's unsuccessful attempts at going back to his roots, be it to folk forms in theatre and music or to miniatures and the Tantric philosophy in painting. Some have seen it as the existence of a plurality of cultures based on Vedic and non-Vedic notions. The Dalit writers and playwrights are questioning the entire literary tradition within which they are writing; to them it is of little or no consequence. For them, the established literary tradition and aesthetic are the high-caste and bourgeois ones. The contradictions for these writers are age-old. They view their writing as standing in the same relationship to the established writing as the Pali *Jatakas* to the latter-day ornate Sanskrit.

It should be clear that this fragmentation is not a mere mirror image of the age-old conflict between the Sanskrit (the cultivated) and the Prakrit (the uncultivated). This fragmentation has a modern aspect which we cannot comprehend without first understanding capitalism and the relations of exploitation typical of that mode of production. Further, imperialism imposes an international aesthetic order of its own and whose impact a Dalit writer, writing in the far corner of Marathwada, cannot escape although he may not be conscious of coming under its influence.

The implications of some of the problems of the new aesthetic order are quite obvious. The liberal aesthetic that dominates the established literary tradition poses a form and content contradiction which is typical of capitalism. In an article defending *War and Peace*, Tolstoy said:

> What is *War and Peace*? It is not a novel, nor is it a poem, still less an historical chronicle. *War and Peace* is what the author wanted and could express in the form in which it was expressed. Such a declaration of disregard by the author for the conventional forms of prose-fiction might have seemed over-confident, had it not been deliberate.[5]

The organic relationship between form and content was self-evident to him. If what an author wishes to express involves 'disregard' for conventional forms, such disregard not only is necessary but ought to be deliberate. However, this organic relationship between form and content, this insistence that what you wish to say should and does determine *how* you say it, is no longer self-evident. It cannot be. The social reality which might have produced the work is internal to it but the beauty or excellence has to be external. Otherwise the commodity will not sell. The fragmentation of any social experience also follows the same lines. The production of art and the marketing of art are two separate functions, each with its own laws. The fragmentation is, thus, complete.

It is the inability to view this fragmentation in its totality, in its modern incarnation, that explains why we have no critical aesthetic theory, no adequate critical writing and debate.

3

Part of the reason for that may be that we in India have not yet realized how 'capitalism' is hostile towards art. Lukács explained the hostility toward art and the place of the modern artist in capitalism thus:

> . . . since such tendencies (especially oppression and exploitation of man by man) attain such a level of inhumanity in no other society as under capitalism . . . every true artist, every true writer as a creative individual is instinctively an enemy of this distortion of the principle of humanism, whether consciously or not.[6]

At no point in history were the arts and the artists so placed. The contributions of capitalism to the arts are rather limited. John Berger, in *Ways of Seeing*, provides a compelling argument for the view that the history of oil-painting needs to be understood in terms of its relation to the rise of capitalism and its expression of the way of seeing the world of the ruling class.[7] The other contribution is the cinema which, in India (I mean the consumerist cinema) in any case, has become a good example of Ruskin's aphorism: 'Industry without art is brutality'.[8]

Anyway, the contradiction between the artist and the social formation was never so acute; the social and political contradictions are becoming sharper every day and the arts are no exception to this. The fragmentation that the sensitive individual perceives around him is indeed the 'distortion of the humanistic principle' that Lukács wrote about. The fragmentation is manifold, its complexities, mind-boggling. This does not mean and should not be interpreted to mean that it is an entirely inexplicable phenomenon. The 'no-exit' view of reality which has come to dominate a lot of our 'modernist' writing and art is invalid not only because it is a pose, a transplant of a late-capitalist European experience onto a semi-feudal, early-capitalist society, but also because the 'no-exit' theory itself does not see the relationship between social reality and creativity quite clearly. It accepts the 'distortion of the humanist principle' as an immutable and unalterable law. The net result is an absurdist view of society, of history, of reality.

In the fragmentation that obtains in India, the artists and writers who find themselves on the side of the oppressed and the exploited have an important legacy to uphold. Beginning with the writings of the twenties and the thirties and the Indian People's Theatre Association (IPTA) movement of the forties, a significant Indian tradition in the arts has been revived, namely the tradition of the arts as a movement. Those who restored this tradition found themselves up against the by no means insignificant influence of British pre-War journals like *Scrutiny* which was against turning experience into 'ideology's homeland',[9] and *Encounter* in the post-War years. The influence of these journals and of the men connected with them (from F. R. Leavis to Stephen Spender) had led many literary and art theoreticians to believe that art and culture were independent entities; to attribute to them a social or an ideological function was tantamount to a violation of their sovereignty. We have had our own versions of *Scrutiny* and *Encounter* in the Indian languages as well as in English. Their mediocrity was not their only weak point. Those who managed these journals were unaware of Indian history and the fact that all art has flourished as a movement, a fact that is certainly true of the past two thousand years of Indian history. The famous cave-temples of western India (the first at Bhaja dating to the second century BC) were a product of a popular and strong Buddhist movement which was a revolt against brahmanism. The early poetry in most Indian languages was a direct product of the Bhakti movement. The Indian artist has always viewed himself as a part of a 'long revolution'.[10] Indian art and writing since the thirties, the more powerful of them that is, have been a product of the anti-imperialist movement, and so on. Indian tradition, thus, has been a markedly ideological one and Indian art has always had something to say. Not only that but those who created it did so with the express purpose of conveying something, of building up something. This is not to say that there have been no other traditions. Of course there have been. The point here, however, is that the 'people' dimension has been equally strong. To cite a perhaps not so well-known example from the field of music—the origins of *tappa* singing are very interesting. There were a number of songs which the people of the Punjab used to sing when they moved from one place to another in caravans of camels. Towards the end of the eighteenth century, Ghulam Rasul Khan, a very distinguished vocalist at the Lucknow court, was struck during his travels in the Punjab by the originality and freshness of those songs. He incorporated some of them and their typical style into the classical style and the outcome was the *tappa*.[11] A new form of singing came into existence as a result of interaction with people.

Those who are emphasizing the divided character of our world are not doing anything unusual or unprecedented; they are relating the arts once again to the people. This aspect has a bearing on the hostility to art that is inherent in capitalism. Modern capitalist society imposes loneliness upon men. In fact, this loneliness is a major theme of a lot of new writing and art. Modern society is anti-people. The new artist/protagonist we have been talking about, however, wants a dialogue. He believes words, colours, gestures, all have a meaning; and that communication is possible. What the critical aesthetic theory has failed to do is explain why communication appears to be impossible. It must be able to explain not only the predicament of this protagonist but also deal with the fact that he—as the representative of a whole class of people, in a manner of speaking—is a result of the fragmentation.

4

Against this background one should look at the concept of progress. The crucial question is *not* whether there is progress in art. The more relevant formulation is that there is a view of progress which goes into the making of art. Victor Hugo said, in *Les Miserables*, 'The real title of this drama is: Progress'.[12] In other words, worthwhile art involves *within itself* the notion of progress. This is the reason why Lenin said, 'Tolstoy is original, because the sum total of his views taken as a whole happens to express the specific features of our revolution as a *peasant* bourgeois revolution' (emphasis as in original). He thought of Tolstoy as 'the mirror of the Russian Revolution'.[13] One may mention here, in passing, Solzhenytsin's view of *War and Peace.* In *August 1914,* Solzhenytsin attributes the failure of the Russian Generals on the eastern front, particularly in the battle of Tennenberg, to their reading of the romanticized version of Kutuzov's campaign in Tolstoy's novel. The net result: the disastrous defeat of 1917, leading to the creation of the Soviet state! In short, if the notion of progress is absent in one's consideration of art, this is where one lands up.

Fragmentation and contradiction are the preoccupation of the artist. These will be increasingly sharpened in view of the fact that economic and political structures in our country are not particularly stable and are not likely to stay stable either. In post-Independence India, these contradictions were articulated around the seventies. The economic and political crisis that this country is living through also dates from that period. Balzac had said of Napoleon that his example was fatal to the nineteenth century 'because of the pretensions it inspires in so many mediocrities'.[14] It would seem that Balzac was wrong in assuming that Napoleon's example was fatal *only* for the nineteenth century.

In such a situation it is small wonder that some writers are talking in their works not of an 'I' but rather of a 'we'. What gives their work a distinct character is their emphasis on 'our' experience. Brecht left an unfinished play called *The Story of the Egotist Johann Fatzer.* The play is about an egotist in a world where individualism has become an obsolete idea.[15] We still have some egotist Fatzers around, no doubt. But it is becoming quite clear that 'our' experience is more relevant and plainly just more interesting in artistic terms than 'my' experience. The need for a critical aesthetic theory is all the greater today precisely because the central question now is: who are the 'we' and who are the 'they'? There has not been adequate discussion *among* the Indian artists on this question at all.

First published in The Truth Unites: Essays in Tribute to Samar Sen (*Calcutta, 1985*)

Notes

1 As quoted in Albert School, *La Revolution Française* (Paris, 1965), p. 9. Translation from the French by Kalindi Deshpande.

2 This distinction is based on Edward W. Said, *Orientalism* (London, 1978).

3 Ibid. p. 32.

4 This is a notion which Raymond Williams defines in his 'Culture and Revolution: A Response', in Terry Eagleton and Brian Wicker, eds., *From Culture to Revolution* (London, 1968), p. 308. There, the idea presumably has a futuristic meaning as the 'common culture' would be realizable in a society 'whose values are at once commonly created . . . and where the discussions and exclusions of class may be replaced by the reality of common and equal membership. That, still, is the idea of a common culture'. Of course, its futuristic character does not make it any less ambiguous or abstract.

5 Leo Tolstoy, 'A Few Words about the Book "War and Peace"', in *Russian Archive* (Moscow, 1868), NO. 3, reproduced in A. V. Knowles, ed., *Tolstoy: The Critical Heritage* (London, 1978), p. 125.

6 Georg Lukács, *Writer and Critic* (London, 1978), p. 69.

7 The summary of John Berger's view is from Leslie Johnson, *Cultural Critics* (Canada, 1979), p. 160.

8 As cited in Anand K. Coomaraswamy, *Selected Papers*, VOL. 2 in Roger Lipsey, ed., *Metaphysics* (Princeton, 1977).

9 Terry Eagleton, *Criticism and Ideology* (London, 1976), p. 15.

10 The term belongs to Raymond Williams. His book of that name was published in 1961 (London).

11 Keshavrao Bhole, *Astal* (in Marathi), a collection of essays on music (Bombay, 1962), p. 21.

12 As quoted in Mary McCarthy, *Ideas and the Novel* (London, 1980), p. 40.

13 See Lenin's article, 'Leo Tolstoy as the Mirror of the Russian Revolution' in his *Collected Works* (Moscow, 1973), VOL. 15, pp. 202–209.

14 As quoted by McCarthy, *Ideas and the Novel*, p. 71.

15 This play is one of those 'fragments' Brecht left behind. No English translation exists as far as I know. The few scenes which he did complete and his commentary are included in VOL. 7 of his *Collected Works* (Berlin, 1965).

Dialectics of Defeat: Some Reflections on Literature, Theatre and Music in Colonial India

> Now is a phase of fatigue in history and yet here are crowds of men and women engaged in preparation. They yearn for ushering in a new spotless earth in accord with their vision of humanity forging ahead.
>
> —Jibanananda Das

What this essay attempts to do is to take a look at what happened to the aesthetic and creative experiences and urges of the people of India during colonial rule (perhaps we could call it the 'colonial aesthetic experience') and illustrate its points with select examples from three Indian languages. What follows, therefore, is *not* a literary history of modern India. Rather, it is an attempt to identify some trends and tendencies in Indian literature and theatre which owe their origins to the colonial experience. The three language areas I have kept in view for the purpose of my argument are Bangla, Hindi and Marathi. However, it is my belief that the tendencies discussed are not limited only to these languages; they must be no less visible and marked in other areas and languages too. The only difference might be chronological as it is, for example, in the case of the three discussed here. The dates of the first 'modern' plays in Indian languages might vary. In fact, they do but that has more to do with the time of the British taking over a given area under their imperial wings. Otherwise, the aesthetic and creative experience of the Indian people during the colonial period shows remarkable similarities. (There are, no doubt, differences as well but they lie outside the scope of this essay.)

An attempt has been made in the following argument to keep the number of author-names and titles to a minimum. At times, important writers or poets have been left out—Jibanananda Das or Hari Narayan Apte would have naturally featured in any literary history but, as explained earlier, this essay does not claim to be such a one. It is also possible that other commentators or historians might choose different or better examples. My essay tries to describe a trend or tendency and examine its connections with and roots in the colonial experience. Thus, the question of which author or playwright best represents that tendency is not very central to my argument.

The scope of this essay has been, in the main, limited to the nineteenth century. References to the twentieth century are not entirely absent but are, essentially, complementary in character. The year 1800 acts as my starting point. The nineteenth century was the high noon of British imperialism and the rule of Queen Victoria (she ascended the throne in 1837) which spans the century, showed in many ways the quintessential characteristics of imperialism. The *bhadralok* of British India tried to imitate Victorian mores and morals. Modernity, capitalism, liberalism and new literary forms came to India in their Victorian avatars. And it was in contra-distinction to the arrogance and ideals of the Victorian age that India's search for a bourgeois sensibility and identity was carried out. Our sensibility did not quite become bourgeois, but that is another matter. The desire or the objective of the new Western-educated elite was certainly to be so for it thought that the non-bourgeois (i.e. non-Western) aim was a crime! Or so it would seem.

1

The singlemost important intervention that colonialism made in the cultural life of India over the last two centuries was the establishment of Fort William College in Calcutta in 1800. Rarely are historical events so obedient to the compulsions of the calendar. Come the nineteenth century and there begins, in the very first year, a new era in the history of Indian literature and theatre, an era of imperial intervention. The College, established by the East India Company to train its administrators in the languages of India, provided facilities for teaching Sanskrit, Arabic, Persian, Hindustani, Bangla, Tamil, Marathi and Kannada. The city of

Calcutta, an obscure little village when the British acquired it in the late seventeenth century, had by then become a major centre of political and economic power. The Empire had spread and the British rulers in Calcutta needed an army of trained administrators who could deal with the natives and their problems in the vernacular and Fort William College was established with that purpose in mind. Close to Calcutta, in Srirampur, missionaries had established the first printing press and begun publishing theological works such as the *Dharma Pustak*, a Bangla translation of the Bible.

Any account of literary movements in colonial India will have to give due credit to the role played by these institutions in the new literature and theatre that grew and developed in the whole of India in the nineteenth century. It was through these institutions that colonialism intervened in the field of arts and literature with far-reaching consequences.

With the decline of Sanskrit as an instrument of cultural expression, several things died out. The most notable casualty was the decline and eventual eclipse of theatre. Works in Sanskrit continued to be written once in a while. Secular aesthetics was not altogether unknown to the Indian tradition, both classical and folk, but it had ceased to make an impact of any significance. The Bhakti movement and the resurgence of poetry it effected from the twelfth to the seventeenth centuries had also been forgotten. By the end of the eighteenth century, Bhakti poetry was no longer read *as* poetry or even as poetry of the revolt against brahmanism which, in fact, is what it was. A strange lapse of memory had occurred. Poets like Tukaram or Kabir were now being interpreted as writers of 'devotional poetry'. A measure of the decline of Sanskrit criticism can be seen in a figure like Madhusudan Saraswati, critic and contemporary of Akbar and Tulsidas, whose work on the rasa theory pleaded for the inclusion of the Bhakti in the rasas but whose discussion of the Bhakti rasa made no reference to Tulsidas, his contemporary and easily the most well-known of the Bhakti poets of north India or 'Hindusthan', as it was then called. Literary criticism thus had become a dead enterprise well before colonial rule came to India.

British intervention in the field of literature, therefore, could not have come at a more appropriate time. Fort William College began its work by standardizing the languages it was teaching—it first compiled and published dictionaries in those languages. Not that there were no dictionaries in the Indian languages but the development of dictionaries is partly a function of any language which must serve as the language of administration, statecraft and so on. British rule contributed to the growth of the Indian vernaculars by turning them into useful and usable instruments of statecraft. With the exception of Marathi during the Maratha ascendancy in western India, no Indian language was used as an official language throughout the medieval period of Indian history. That situation changed with the British. The dominance of Persian in most parts of northern India as the language of high culture and high administration finally came to an end. The British started schools in the native languages, a matter in which the Bombay Presidency seems to have taken the lead—by the middle of the nineteenth century there were more Marathi medium schools in Maharashtra than ever. Fort William College also worked on rendering the *Hitopades*, the *Panchatantra*, the *Vetal Panchavimsati* and other popular Sanskrit works into Indian vernaculars. In so doing, the pandits in its monopoly opened new vistas before the 'natives' in the use of their languages. It looked as if the colonialists had seen the wisdom of the ancient Indian *vyakarana* formulation *saktam padam* ('the word is powerful'; some liberty has been taken in this translation. It was possible and necessary as the *sutra* is clearly taken out of its context. Besides, *slesha* is a permissible literary device after all!) and had decided to master the native word with a view to dominating the native. But it was not a one-way traffic. Dominance and loot constitute the essence of imperialism. At the same time, it is also true that, domestically, new kinds of economic relations were being introduced. The colonial state was very unlike any earlier form of state that the Indian people had known. India was forced into a new era. To describe this era as an era of modernity is not really saying much. What happened during the colonial phase was that 'different sides of the great geopolitical divide . . . two worlds and "two histories" '[1]—to use Perry Anderson's phrase (used by him in a different context, of course)—confronted each other. This confrontation was bound to have as strange and unlikely results as the confrontation itself.

On the cultural plane, the contradictory nature of the results was the most obvious. A sensitive mind was reacting to things European, at times with great enthusiasm, at times with defiance but, most often, with a mixture of both. Nowhere else is this mixed response as clearly visible as in literature and theatre. The literary movements of nineteenth-century India vividly reveal the fact that the various phenomena within a movement quite often evince contradictory manifestations. The Indian elite's relationship with colonialism is one such case and our literature and theatre demonstrate that better than any other.

The impact of English was so thorough that even the syntax of Indian languages underwent a change. There is a book aptly entitled 'The English Incarnation of Marathi Prose'.[2] To cite just one example: a sentence such as 'I told him that I would meet him at 7 p.m.' was unknown to traditional Marathi speech. Ordinarily, a speaker of Marathi always said: 'I would meet him at 7 p.m., I told him'. Or 'I do not see the sight which you see' would become, in traditional Marathi speech, 'You are seeing a sight I do not see' and so on. Sentence-structure and modes of speech changed and it is interesting to see how the traditional forms of address changed as well.

The colonial experience made us aware of 'culture' as a separate world of discourse. No Indian language had a specific term for 'culture' before colonization. This obviously did not mean that there was no culture but that culture as an autonomous world of discourse did not exist. Everything was dharma. Going to a temple was dharma, singing a raga or a ragini was also dharma. Dharma in this context not meaning religion but indicating a space which an individual creates or obtains in a given area—action, duty or creation. A space which was part of the whole, a continuous space. Hence, such diverse actions as singing, worshipping or procreating were all described as dharma. It was a secular concept except that its secular meaning is not as relevant to this discussion as the fact that it allowed discontinuities in discourse. The encounter with colonialism and, through it, with capitalism brought us the world of autonomous cultural discourse. The word *sanskriti,* commonly used for culture in almost all Indian languages is, in fact, an invention of the colonial era. The other word being proposed at that time was *kristi.* Loosely translated, it would mean 'cultivation' and would be a near-exact translation of the German *bildung.* It is not that there was no history to the word *sanskriti.* There was. The *Aitereya Brahmana* refers to begetting progeny also as *silpa* (the art of sculpture), hence as *samskara.*[3] At any rate, Rabindranath Tagore preferred *sanskriti* to *kristi* partly because of these roots and, partly, because *kristi* (unlike its meaning in classical Sanskrit) meant the five *jaatis* or sub-groups of the Aryans, the *panchakrstayah,* namely Anu, Druhu, Turwas, Yadu and Puru.[4] Suniti Kumar Chatterji drew Tagore's attention to the usage of the word *sanskrit* in Marathi (sometime in 1922) in the sense of culture.[5] Be that as it may, finding words for anything is to define it. An attempt was made to define 'culture', define the limits of cultural discourse and its autonomy. In a sense, the European occupation forced us to define several things and cultural discourse was one of them. Whether it is Tagore or Acharya Javdekar or Acharya Hazari Prasad Dwivedi, several Indian intellectuals and writers have at different times commented upon 'culture' and the proper Indian word for it.

As I have mentioned earlier, the linguistic experience of the Indian people underwent a change during this period. It was, of course, different in different areas. In north India, the colonial period marked the final emergence of Hindi with the Devanagari script as the language of cultural expression. Ronald Stuart McGregor has succinctly described the phenomenon:

> While Hindustani and Persian might serve the East Indian Company as languages of commerce and law, it was realized by some that there would henceforth be a

> role in north India for another form of language which should not rely as heavily as Hindustani on Persian and Arabic vocabulary, but should approximate more nearly in vocabulary and cultural affiliation to the various regional and local dialects spoken by the mass of population and should be written in the Devanagari script. Perhaps Brijbhasa itself might serve but given the currency of the Delhi speech (sometimes referred to as 'Khari Boli') it was inevitable that the latter should become the basis of the new language, Sanskritic rather than Persian in cultural affiliation, *not 'created by the British' but owing its main development to new conditions brought about by their presence,* which begins to come into prominence in the early nineteenth century . . . (emphasis added).[6]

The case of the emergence of Hindi has been cited because quite unwittingly the colonial initiative contributed to the process of forging the dialects in the north Indian region into a language capable of modern, cultural expression. This was true of other Indian languages as well. The early nineteenth-century writers—at least some of them—gave the British more credit for it than they deserved. See, for example, what Ramkamal Sen had to say in his preface to his Bangla-English Dictionary (1830):

> Whatever has been done towards the revival of the Bengali language, its improvement and in fact the establishment of it as a language, must be attributed to that excellent man Carey and his colleagues.[7]

Carey was professor of Bangla and Sanskrit at Fort William College. In short, the credit which Sen wished to attribute to Carey was, in fact, by *lakshana* (suggested meaning) being attributed to British rule.

2

That was, however, not the only 'creditable' aspect of the colonial cultural experience. Formalization of the modern language occurred through the prominence that prose acquired in Indian literature during this period. Prose traditions were not entirely absent in vernacular literatures in pre-colonial times—in Marathi, the beginnings of the literary tradition are associated with the prose writing of the *Mahanubhavas* (twelfth century AD). In Hindi or Bangla, however, prose writing really begins with the colonial period. Pre-colonial literary expression was necessarily in poetry which is, partly, due to the oral tradition which has dominated Indian civilization. With the printing press, prose became a feasible mode of cultural expression. The first half of the nineteenth century is the period when prose styles emerge in different Indian languages. With writers like Krishnashastri Chiplunkar and his son Vishnushastri (in Marathi) and Rammohun Roy (in Bangla), prose became 'the vehicle of philosophic exposition and religious and social polemic'.[8] There is some point in putting the Chiplunkars—father and son—and Rammohun Roy together because they represent opposite poles of the polemical debate that began with Roy and reached its high point in Jotirao Phule.

Jotirao Phule, who died in 1880, is only now attracting historians' attention, which is a pity. Phule, unlike Rammohun Roy who was for reformed Vedantism, was a complete rebel against the brahmanical tradition and had an organic link with the social ethos that the low-caste Marathi Bhakti poetry represented. Modern Indian historiography has ignored this man until very recently and the commonly heard Dalit criticism—that the high-caste, English-educated historians felt at home with the positions taken and the reforms advocated by people like Roy and Agarkar but would not touch a *kunbi* (low peasant) like Phule with a barge pole—is not entirely baseless. The Dalit critics do not underestimate the contribution of Roy and others but they might prefer to believe that Phule, rather than Roy, 'is one of those great men who are born at a critical moment in their country's history, and who shape its destiny'.[9]

One may or may not share the view about the *bhadralok* preference for somebody of their stock. It is, however, true that, beginning roughly in the middle of the nineteenth century, prose not only became a vehicle of philosophic exposition but also the incisive record of the 'diagnosis of our time'. The essay of that name by Karl Mannheim begins thus:

> Let us take the attitude of a doctor who tries to give a scientific diagnosis of the illness from which we all suffer. There is no doubt that our society has been taken ill. What is the disease, and what would be its cure? If I had to summarise the situation in a single sentence I would say: 'We are living in an age of transition . . .'[10]

In a way, Roy and Phule were also talking of transition except that they were not uncertain about it, unlike Mannheim. On the contrary, they were looking forward to it. This is the reason why, even in their sharpest polemics, the early social reformers and the essayists are optimistic. Looking back, the most striking quality of Indian vernacular prose, whether of Roy or Agarkar or Phule, is the general sense of optimism that seems to underlie their writing. Agarkar, Phule and Roy are critical of society and quite ruthless in their diagnoses but they are never pessimistic about the future of that society. They are the men of vision Jibanananda Das talks about in his poem cited at the start of this essay. Phule is, in fact, militantly optimistic. He was the first Indian to have introduced peasantry as a class in his writing which Rosalind O'Hanlon has discussed at some length in her recent study of Mahatma Jotirao Phule and low-caste protest in nineteenth-century western India.[11] His most eloquent piece discusses what the peasants can do about their miserable lot and exploitation, entitled 'The Whip of the Peasantry' (*Setkaryacha Asud*). Phule thought in caste terms but his concern about caste was not limited to protesting against the *homo hierarchichus* that the caste system postulated. He was talking about *homo econominc*us but in terms of the *varnas*. His literary output has remained largely ignored because of the *bhadralok* dominance of our historiography. Otherwise it would have been easy to see that he was India's first 'radical' playwright, essayist and poet. Even the 'left' criticism has failed to come to terms with the 'militant optimism' of Phule's writing. In a way, colonialism, and the fact that

Phule was not as fiercely anti-imperialist as Tilak, might have been responsible for it. Be that as it may, the colonial experience made the Indian intellectual and writer aware of the movement of history. Phule represents its most important example because, as a representative of the lower castes and classes in the latter half of the nineteenth century, he saw the inevitable change in our society and how British imperialism was historically playing a progressive role. He articulated the dialectics of defeat. He had no use for the liberals' enthusiasm for British rule and, at the same time, saw vividly the limitations of the orthodox nationalist programme.[12]

The encounter with the West seems to have produced quite a spectrum of attitudes and responses both towards the West and towards India. Michael Madhusudan Dutt represents a typical case of the confusion and the bewildering responses of the time. This talented playwright and poet, to whom one can safely attribute the credit of writing the first genuinely modern play in India (*Sarmistha*, 1858), was even doubtful about writing in Bangla. He wrote some rather tepid verse in English but, before long, discovered that his writing in English made no impact on anyone. His enthusiasm for things Western was so extraordinary that he wrote of his favourite poet Milton: 'Nothing can be better than Milton . . . I don't think it is possible to equal Virgil, Kalidas and Tasso. Though glorious, still they are mortal poets. Milton is divine'.[13]

This comparison of Milton with the ancient Indian poet Kalidas is interesting in view of what Warren Hastings had said in his letter to Nathaniel Smith on the *Bhagwad Gita*.

> It will not be fair to try its relative worth by a comparison with the original text of the first standards of European composition; but let these be taken even in the most esteemed of their prose translations and in that equal scale let their merits be weighed. I should not fear to place in opposition to the best French versions of the most admired passages of the Iliad or Odyssey, or of the *first and the sixth books of our own Milton, highly as I venerate the latter*, the English translation of the *Mahabharata* (emphasis added).[14]

Hastings wrote that letter in 1784. Dutt's remark belongs to the late fifties of the nineteenth century. More than two hundred years after Hastings' letter it is easy to see that he was closer to the truth than Dutt. But that was because Hastings wrote from a position of colonial dominance and, hence, could take a more detached view of the two traditions involved. Dutt was a victim of the colonial situation that was bound to lead to a sceptical attitude towards his own inheritance. His conversion to Christianity itself or his claim that he was writing Indian mythology in the Greek style showed his ambivalence towards the Indian tradition. The nineteenth-century intellectual writer was caught between the two tendencies of either rejection of or excessive glorification of that tradition. It is doubtful if the East and West really met in the nineteenth century. It is my opinion that they confronted each other. Michael Madhusudhan Dutt and Vishnushastri Chiplunkar represent the two mutually opposite types of writers that this confrontation produced.

There were also interesting parallels between the European attitudes of the nineteenth century and the Indian ones. It was an age of the new. The words *nava, navin* or *nutan* (all meaning new) seem to dominate the thinking of the intellectuals and writers of the nineteenth century. Compare this to Holbrook Jackson's assessment: in *The Eighteen Nineties,* he characterized the period as typified by books titled *The New Hedonism* and *The New Fiction* and by movements calling themselves 'New Paganism', 'New Voluptuousness' and, in obvious reaction, 'New Remorse' but also 'New Spirit', 'New Humour', 'New Realism', 'New Drama', to say nothing of 'New Unionism' and 'New Woman'.[15] This is not to suggest that the Indian 'new' was the same as the European 'new' of the late nineteenth century. They could not have been. The latter was the 'new' of the bourgeois experience, the 'new' of the triumphant powers and peoples. The Indian 'new' was the 'new' of the defeated, colonized people. But the search for the 'new' becomes inevitable when you become a part of the process of capitalisation (clearly in an extended and secondary way).

The critique of society also takes forms which are, at times, comparable to those made by the European critics. Agarkar wrote more than five essays on 'the dress of our menfolk' in the 1880s. His discussion of the Indian dress (prevalent among the upper-caste Maharashtrians of the time) was not very friendly or appreciative.[16] Had he been a novelist he would have made his character dismiss it in much the same way as Marcel Proust had his dandified Block renounce the watch and the umbrella as 'insipid bourgeois implements'.[17] Agarkar's critique of the headgear, the coat and jacket of his contemporaries in Pune is, of course, in different terms. Nevertheless, the parallels are striking. Different perspectives emerge from the different positions that an essayist like Agarkar in a colonial society occupied and a novelist like Proust in France did. But the newly educated Hindu in nineteenth-century India was in a self-critical mood. His self-criticism, like that of 'many bourgeois' of nineteenth-century Europe, as Peter Gay has pointed out, turned itself into 'self-laceration'. This may, perhaps, explain the contemporary Hindu revivalism in India and the high tide of conservatism in western Europe.

Very much like the bourgeoisie in nineteenth-century Europe, the educated Hindu of that generation indulged in, to use Peter Gay's words again, 'collective denunciations with an aridity that would have done honour to a tribe of masochists'.[18] This led to the phenomenon which George Bernard Shaw very aptly described in his preface to Dickens' *Hard Times* in 1912: 'The first half of the nineteenth century considered itself the greatest of all centuries. The second discovered that it was the wickedest'. In India, the time frame was different but the reversal of estimates was almost similar. A tradition created by Keshab Chandra Sen or M. G. Ranade, Dutt or Agarkar or Phule was replaced by the one created by Bankimchandra Chatterjee and Vishnushastri Chiplunkar. The 'new' thought was considered to be the greatest in the early part of our colonial experience. Before long it was discovered to be the wickedest.

This was, partly, to be expected. As in Europe, in India too 'the triumphs of the new, of the secular, of science were far from complete and undisputed'. In 1895, Emile Durkheim could deplore these times of 'renascent mysticism'.[19] Rabindranath Tagore, Keshavsut and Premchand represented the high point of Indian creativity being truly universal. On the whole, these are exceptions which prove the rule: in a colonial society, understanding the specificity of the colonial situation and thus establishing and reasserting identity were the main objectives of creative pursuit.

This may be the reason why the novel as a genre never really took off in India. Again, Tagore, Bankimchandra, Premchand and Ketkar could be cited as great novelists. Yet it would be true to say that the Indian novel really comes into its own in post-colonial times. Lukács argued that the novel was the genre of the bourgeois epoch. It is doubtful if in a colonized society one can actually speak of a proper bourgeois epoch. Indian literatures boasted of various forms of narrative which were fascinating and varied. What is not clear is whether they could be described as novels proper. The nineteenth- and early twentieth-century Indian novel was closer to traditional narrative than the polyphonic novel that Bakhtin talked of. Balzac, in a famous statement in the preface to *La Comédie Humaine*, asserted that he wanted to compete with civil society, not simply 'represent' it.[20] The Indian novel has remained largely representational. There has been highly interesting work done lately on Bankimchandra and Ketkar. The insights that these works provide on the fiction of these writers are very useful. Yet they do not quite establish them as creators of modern fiction which represents 'a problematic hero whose ideals were more or less systematically contradicted by social reality' or as works similar to those of 'critical realists like Balzac and Tolstoy' which 'disclose dimensions of contemporary history that challenged their own explicit ideologies'.[21] In aesthetic terms, the Indian bourgeois sensibility is scarcely fifty years old. In earlier times, it rose to these heights only in bits and flashes. That is the reason, perhaps, why the Indian short story offered richer fare than the Indian novel. Our great novels have been a proto-history of the novel. The history has just begun.

It might be useful to refer to the fact that some contemporary observers of the literary scene had seen the limitations of the

Indian novel. A good example of this is the essay on the novel that Rajwade wrote in 1905. He was highly critical of the contemporary Indian novel and had even suggested that Indian novelists do not understand 'realism' and that they do not see the distinction between 'natural' and 'realistic'.[22]

In poetry, however, extraordinary heights were reached. Rabindranath Tagore is the most well-known example and hardly needs any elaboration here. The romantic tradition in Indian poetry has been quite strong. Modern Indian poetry begins with Madhusudan Dutt. In terms of form this extraordinary man made many experiments. He was the first to write sonnets in any Indian language. He was also the first to have discovered the music of the blank verse. His compositions in the traditional *matra vrttas* (Sanskrit variation of the rhymed verse) are not insignificant. In Hindi, Marathi and Bangla, like in other languages of India, poetry took to newer forms, the sonnet and blank verse being the most notable ones. Romantic verse became popular towards the end of the nineteenth century. In Marathi, for example, the most glorious period of romantic poetry comes to an end sometime in 1920. This romanticism was, however, marked by despair—images of darkness, long endless nights, loneliness and pessimism. There were a few exceptions such as Tagore or Keshavsut whose poetry rose above this. Some critics might doubt even that because they think that such imagery was a necessary part of the poets' craft and creativity. One volume of criticism discussing such poetry (in Marathi) was entitled *Andhar Yatra* (journey into darkness).[23] A defeated people were articulating their romanticism. It could have only been the romanticism of despair. The dialectics of defeat result in a co-existence of despair and romanticism. One has not seen (*Andhar Yatra* included) much writing on the end-century romantics which places their romantic despair in the context of our colonial experience.

What sustained our poetry was the fact that the bulk of Indian writing had been in poetic terms. It was a genre with the longest and the most productive history in our literatures. The result was that the new poet in India was on firmer ground when he attempted poetry. His colonial experience in a peculiar way contributed to his search for the reasons for his despair. There is a short essay by Rahul Sankrityayan on Bharatendu Harishchandra called *Bharatendu aur Pushkin.*[24] The thrust of Sankrityayan's argument is to compare the rebellious spirit of the two poets. If Bharatendu was worried about the *Bharat durdasha,* Pushkin was worried about the decline of Russia, its backwardness. He was pained as much as any Indian of the colonial times was, to have to argue that Russia had a history. Sankrityayan's observations (which can be extended to many poets in other Indian languages) are not important because of the parallels and similarities he sees in the poetry of the two men which may be dismissed as purely coincidental. (He, in fact, finds it interesting that both men lived rather short lives.) It is even doubtful if Bharatendu had ever read Pushkin; he could not have. Rahul's observations are important because he has related the work of the two poets to the states in which they found their country.

One can, perhaps, take the argument one step ahead. Indian poetry of the nineteenth and the early twentieth century was an expression of a damaged civilization. Imperialism introduced new forms, new modes of expression but it never completely integrated the aesthetic of the new Indian literature with its own. It could not have. This is more apparent in the poetry of the colonial period than perhaps in any other form of literature.

3

Drama was another area where the colonial age introduced and contributed several new, hitherto unknown, forms. In fact, it was an enterprising Russian gentleman, one Lebedeff, who produced the first 'modern' play in English in Calcutta on November 11, 1795. It appears that there was a second performance of this play on March 21, 1796.[25] The first modern play by an Indian was also in English—K. M. Banerji wrote 'a play in a western manner', *The Persecuted,* in 1832.[26] Soon after, however, theatre activity began in the Presidency areas. Prasanna Kumar Tagore founded the Hindu Natak Mandali in December 1831. Balsastri Jambhekar wrote an editorial note in the first ever Marathi periodical *Darpana* (founded by him in 1832) welcoming the Mandali.[27]

The first Marathi 'modern' play by Vishnudas Bhave went on stage on November 3, 1843. Lakshman Simha translated *Shakuntala* in 1863 and may have been indebted in this enterprise to Iswarchandra Vidyasagar's Bangla prose translation of the same which was published in 1854.[28] The Marathi and Malayalee *Shakuntala* went on stage in 1880.

Understandably, Shakespeare seems to have provided a major source for early translators. *Hamlet, Macbeth, Othello, The Merchant of Venice* seem to have been particularly popular. Likewise, Sanskrit plays provided another inexhaustible source.

Perhaps because of the strong tradition of folk and regional theatre, drama easily became the most prestigious and popular form. In the course of his brief lifetime, Bharatendu Harishchandra wrote close to two score plays, both translations and originals. Right from the beginning of modern Indian drama, folk and classical forms have dominated the mode of dramatic composition. Strangely, Sahasrabuddhe traces the history of Marathi drama from 1880 (the date of Kirloskar's *Shakuntala* going on stage) because he thought that Bhave's plays did not represent modern drama—Bhave's plays mixed 'elements from *bharud, tamasha, lalit, dasavatara* and so on'.[29] This is the most extraordinary statement to make; not only because it does injustice to Bhave but also because it postulates a misplaced contradiction between traditional forms of theatre and modern drama. The exact opposite of this attitude was heard by this author in a seminar in Delhi where a former official of the Sangeet Natak Akademi claimed credit for introducing and adopting folk forms for the use of modern theatre. The process had begun a good one hundred and forty years before the official's words. Even Kirloskar, who according to Sahasrabuddhe is the first genuine modern playwright, did the same. Bharatendu used forms like *bhana* and *satta-*

ka in the nineteenth century but in his plays, although the dialogues were in Hindi, the verse was in dialect, presumably the Brajbhasa. After all, Lalluji Lal, one of the founders of modern Hindi diction, said in 1808: 'Everyone speaks Brajbhasa, it is as great as Sanskrit. All poets use it. They think it to be the source of the great rasa'.[30] It would appear that even in Bharatendu's time the Hindi play was, linguistically, a mixed affair.

Over the years theatre acquired a major political significance. Many writers attempted to use theatre in the anti-imperialist struggle. Khadikar, whose important works were penned from the 1890s to about the mid-1920s, was an immensely popular and gifted playwright. He also became a political playwright. Quite a few of his plays were banned and he was jailed a number of times. The use of allegory, satire, recreation and reinterpretation of history in modern, nationalist terms became a feature of Indian playwriting.

At the same time, from the 1870s onwards, Indian theatre showed a remarkable range of formal experimentation. On the one hand, traditional forms like Dasavatara or Yakshagana contributed to the richness of fare along with Sanskrit forms like *prahasana* or *bhana*. On the other, Parsi theatre, which became popular after the 1870s with its rich and complex narrative and influences of Marathi and Gujarati theatre, generally tended towards a very dazzling spectacle and a good plot. Manmohan Basu, in his play on Harishchandra written in 1875, went fairly close to the Jatra form. Natyasangeet, so very popular on the Marathi stage, will be mentioned later. But its role in formal experimentation should not be undermined.

In the first years of the twentieth century, theatre had become quite popular and we even have playwrights living off their work. G. B. Deval may well be the first Indian playwright who went to a court of law to establish his royalty rights and actually won the case! Admittedly, it is in the twentieth century that Bangla and Marathi theatre reach their high point, a period which has not been covered in this essay. The excellence of a Tagore or a Khadilkar is seen essentially in the twentieth century (although

Tagore's first play was written in 1881 and Khadilkar's in 1891). But by the turn of the century, modern theatre had come to stay and was a flourishing tradition in Maharashtra and Bengal.

In many ways, modern theatre was the Indian's attempt to come to terms with his heritage and to face the situation created by colonialism and the new ideas and bad effects that it generated. Thus Bharatendu attacked the hypocrisy of the brahmanical society in his plays like *Vaidki Hinsa Hinsa na Bhavati* and Deval attacked the practice of marrying off young girls to elderly men in his *Sarada.*

In short, theatre became a vehicle through which the modern Indian discovered his self, his tradition, philosophical positions and also the political and philosophical meaning of existence. In addition, 'modern' theatre helped (decades before the Sangeet Natak Akademi was born) the traditional forms to survive. Just as modern industry ruined the indigenous handicrafts in our country, modern theatre and, later, cinema could have done the same. But that did not happen. In terms of music, acting styles, content, amalgamation of different forms and variety of concerns—social, political and philosophical—of the playwrights, modern Indian drama came of age in the twentieth century. The active drama movements, at least in some parts of the country, were also a function of the assertion of identity of those people—whether in Bengal or Maharashtra or Kerala.

4

Assertion of identity and retrieval of a cultural tradition are best exemplified by the popularity and spread of Hindustani (north Indian) classical music outside north India where *gharanas* (schools) of Hindustani music are based. This is not to say that Hindustani music was not already popular in outlying areas like Maharashtra or Bengal. Indeed, the Peshwa court in Pune patronized visiting vocal classical singers from north India in the eighteenth century. What happened in the nineteenth century was that we now had major practitioners of music, i.e. vocalists and instrumentalists, emerging in areas like Maharashtra and Bengal.

In the case of Maharashtra this is particularly notable. Gwalior, in north India, home of one of the *gharanas* of Hindustani music, was ruled by a Maratha family. Yet, prior to the nineteenth century we do not hear of any significant Maharashtrian pandit of music. The tradition of Pune-based musicians begins with the nineteenth century. (This would be true of almost all provinces where Hindustani music is popular, namely Bengal, Gujarat, Orissa and Assam. We see, even in these provinces, major names in Hindustani classical music emerging in the nineteenth century and after.) The popularity has, if anything, increased in the twentieth century. K. L. Bhole, major historian of music and music director of the Prabhat Film Company in the thirties and forties, has recorded that in the late nineteenth century three outstanding names emerged on the Maharashtra musical scene: Balkrishna Buwa Ichalkaranjikar, Ramakrishnabuwa Vaze and Bhaskarbuwa Bakhle.[31] All of them had been to the north and spent several years learning music. They did more than anyone else to popularize Hindustani classical music in Maharashtra. Legend has it that Pandit Bhatkhande, who made the first attempt to transform the essentially oral tradition of music into a written one, was once asked why he was 'writing' the music down. His reply among other things illustrates the point made above: 'Maharashtra does not have much of art. I thought it should at least have science!'

A popular theatre form in Maharashtra was the Tamasha in which the singing depended upon a lyrical form called the *lavani*. Peshwa Bahirao II encouraged a new form of *lavani* which was (like the *khayal gayaki* of the north) sung not in a Tamasha but at the court or sung sitting, unlike the traditional one accompanied by dance. Honaji Bala was the poet who wrote this kind of *lavani* which, however, in formal terms, did not sever its connection with the mainstream *lavani*. In other words, Maharashtra seems to have turned in a significant measure to practising Hindustani music in the colonial age. By and large, it would be true to say that it was at this time that classical Hindustani music became really popular in terms of the number of its practitioners outside of north India. I have always wondered why this was so. One possible explanation could be that although there is a wide variety of art forms and rich classical traditions in pre-capitalist societies like India, these are essentially local in character. If you wanted to study the music of the Agra or Gwalior *gharana,* you had actually to travel there. Classical musicians did travel but the musical traditions did not. It was a bit like localized commodity production. The *gharanas* managed to retain their purity by resisting emigration. With the new political set-up this tradition broke down. The three masters, about who Bhole wrote, came back to Maharashtra and with them began the chapter of Hindustani classical music that the history of Maharashtra had hitherto lacked. The new socio-economic order that colonialism sought to create in the whole of India is partly responsible for this.

Secondly, in Maharashtra at any rate, the elite had just lost political power. In 1818, Pune fell to the British. The Pune brahmans now had to assert their identity in some area other than politics. They turned to culture as a means of doing so. Traditionally, they had, in any case, been the intellectuals. It was not altogether unknown for them to turn away from brahmanical functions. Quite a number of them were landlords and, as such, capable of patronizing art at the local level. The dominance of landlords and absentee landlords in the sphere of arts and aesthetics is partly to be attributed to their being a leisure class of a kind. It is not an accident that the smaller states of the Deccan (allowed to survive by the British) became major centres of musical activity. For example, Miraj became a centre of musical instruments.[32] In the twentieth century, Miraj was famous not only for the sitars it manufactured but also because it was the home of Abdul Karim Khan, the most well-known vocalist of the Kirana *gharana.*

It does seem that the spread and popularity of Hindustani classical music in the nineteenth century (in our century it has, if anything, grown) were a function of this assertion of the Indian cultural identity. A demoralized people who had lost political power was trying to define itself, seek fulfillment for itself in the manifest excellence of the Indian musical tradition and this, understandably, went hand in hand with the more general search for the meaning of India and the Indian tradition. Colonialism and the opposition to it revealed the metaphysics of Indian music. The most notable example in terms of this quest and its fulfilment in music is the experimentation that Rabindranath Tagore did with the ragas resulting in Rabindrasangeet. This is not the place to go into the meaning and importance of Rabindrasangeet. Nor is the present writer competent to do so. There seems little doubt, however, that there is perhaps no better example of modern India coming to terms with the classical tradition not merely in terms of its technical details but also in terms of retrieving the philosophical and aesthetic world of that tradition.

Imperialism forces you to take a look at yourself, to redefine yourself. The aesthetic pursuits of colonized people are for that reason the most fascinating. The aesthetics of music is by its nature resistant to systematic articulation. Indian music has yet to find its Adorno. In any case, what Adorno says might be of interest here. He talks of open forms in music. In the Western tradition he thinks the development of the 'open form' has gone through two stages. Now the Indian musical tradition is essentially one of open forms. The ragas encourage an extraordinary degree of improvisation or even of 'vagueness and oscillations', to borrow Adorno's description of the Motzartian Rondo. I do not mean to suggest that Adorno's account is useful for understanding the developments in Indian music. Reference to his work has been made just to point out that the practitioners of music during colonial times did in fact show 'the intuitive sense of form' (*Formgefuhi*) that Adorno sees in Bach.[33] Tagore's Rabindrasangeet shows us so.

The less well-known and, at times, unduly criticized if not actually maligned formal experimentation in music was the Natyasangeet in Marathi, an adaptation of the classical vocal tradition for use in theatre. During its best period, i.e. from 1880 to 1920, the raga form underwent an aesthetically magnificent change. The raga structure was made to look like a Japanese Bonsai tree. A Natyageet (the lyric in the musical) demonstrated all the features of a raga in encapsulated form; it was raga music rendered self-consciously in a theatrical form. Bal Gandharva, easily the greatest singer-actor Indian theatre has produced, had the intuitive sense of form (*Formgefuhi*) referred to earlier. Kumar Gandharva, the well-known and the most creative of the contemporary vocalists, paid tribute to the master by recording a disc of his renderings of the master's songs. The disc had an apt title: *Mala Umajlele Bal Gandharva* ('Bal Gandharva as I understand him'). Come the twenties and the early creativity of Natyasangeet disappears. Most of the latter-day singers treat Natyasangeet more as an abridged version of the raga rather than as a form in its own right. It is perhaps no coincidence that Bal Gandharva was his adopted name, given to him by no less a person than Lokmanya Tilak—a typical example of the close link between the nationalist movement and the arts. The full significance of Natyasangeet cannot be understood unless one places it against the backdrop of the colonial experience and the search for more meaningful art forms that the experience seems to have entailed.

The most obvious change that colonialism made to our musical taste consisted in the introduction of the gramophone record. It brought Indians face to face or, shall we say, ear to ear with art in what Walter Benjamin has called 'the age of mechanical reproduction'. It is a matter of considerable debate whether this business of 'mechanical reproduction' is altogether a good thing. We need not go into that here except to say that disc music went into the far corners of India in a way in which it had not gone before. Besides, this must have been a unique experience for the average Indian who could now own music. He had owned books. He had owned portraits and paintings. He had owned craft objects. He had never owned music until now. It would be difficult to describe it but a change came over the 'traditional' attitude to music according to which music was played either in a temple or in the court of a king or of a zamindar or in the chambers of courtesans in urban centres. Now it entered the living room. In a caste-based society like India's, this has had tremendous social significance. It would be a permissible overstatement that the interface between Indian sensibility and colonialism gave the musician the kind of social respectability which he did not and could not possess for at least a thousand years. In a sense, the dark ages were over for him.

5

This survey has been rather sketchy and manifestly inadequate. But it gives us some idea of our aesthetic experience during colonial times. We need a theoretical perspective which will bring together, in a systematic way, the aspects mentioned so far. Amilcar Cabral has written in a consistent manner on colonialism and culture. His insight—that 'national liberation' is 'necessarily a cultural act'[34]—is more than borne out by my essay. But his theories cannot be entirely applicable to the situation of colonial India. He had Africa and Portuguese colonialism in mind andcharacterized the African situation thus:

> One of the gravest errors, if not the worst, committed by the colonial powers in Africa was to have ignored or underestimated the cultural strength of African peoples. This attitude was particularly blatant in the case of the Portuguese colonial domination which not only categorically denied the existence of African cultural values . . . but also stubbornly refused to allow any political freedom of expression.[35]

It is easy to see that the description would apply to the colonies of Portugal or France. The nature of the British colonial state was different. Further, unlike in French and Portuguese colonies in Africa or the Carribbean, India had a flourishing indigenous linguistic and literary tradition. There was no question, as Madhusudan Dutt's example demonstrates, of Indian writers becoming, in the main, writers in English. For, a writer in colonial India was not faced with the problem which, for example, Aimé Céssaire was:

> ... for me French was a tool that I wanted to use in developing a new means of expression. I wanted to create an Antillean French, a black Frenchy that, while still being French, had a black character.[36]

Tagore or Khadilkar or Premchand was not creating a 'brown' English. His tool was not and could not have been English. He was an inheritor of a classical literary and musical tradition. This is an important difference. Nor would it be historically accurate to suggest that the West denied the existence of Indian (or, for that matter, Chinese) cultural values. It was interested in reducing those values to a secondary position. These differences, namely, an existence of fairly old literary and linguistic traditions and the inheritance of a classical tradition in the arts make the Indian situation very different. I do not mean to say the things Indian were superior to things African, just to suggest that they were different.

Colonialism in cultural terms was like a period of disturbed sleep for the ancient Indian people. They lost some, they gained some. Colonialism has been a mixed experience as much in the cultural sphere as in the spheres of economy and polity. In India, the defeat at the hands of colonialism has had a dialectics of its own. It resulted in the suppression of the Indian people. At the same time and because of it, it led to the retrieval of cultural classical traditions and languages. That, in sum, was our colonial aesthetic experience which was also an anti-colonial aesthetic *experience.*

First published in Economic and Political Weekly, *12 December 1987*

Notes

An earlier draft of this paper was presented in Leningrad in August 1987 at the Joint Indo-Soviet Seminar organized by the Oriental Institute in Moscow and the Nehru Museum and Library. My thanks are due to Ram Bapat, Prabhat Patnaik, C. P. Chandrasekhar, Anil Bhatti, Utsa Patnaik and Gyanendra Pande who commented upon the earlier draft. Needless to say I alone am responsible for the views expressed in the paper or such errors and mistakes as there might be in it.

1 Perry Anderson, 'Problems of Socialist Strategy' in Perry Anderson and Robin Blackburn, eds., *Towards Socialism* (London, 1965), p. 225.

2 D. V. Potdar, *Marathi Gadyacha Ingraji Avatara* ('The English Incarnation of Marathi Prose'; in Marathi), (Pune, n.d.).

3 Cited in Nihar Ranjan Ray, 'Krsti, Culture evam Sanskrit' in Prabhakar Machwe, ed., *Bharatiya Sanskriti* (in Hindi), (Calcutta, 1983), p. 18.

4 Suniti Kumar Chatterji, 'Sanskrit, Silpa, Itihasa, Jijnasa' (in Bangla) cited in Nihar Ranjan Ray, ibid., p. 1.

5 Ibid., p. 7.

6 Ronald Stuart McGregor, 'Hindi Literature of the 19th Century', FACS. 2 in *Hindi Literature of the Nineteenth and Early Twentieth Centuries* (Wiesbaden, 1974), VOL. 8, p. 63.

7 Cited in J. C. Ghosh, *Bengali Literature* (London, 1949), p. 102.

8 Ghosh, ibid., p. 107.

9 This is Ghosh's description of Rammohun Roy, ibid.

10 Karl Mannheim, *Diagnosis of our Times* (London, 1962), p. 1.

11 R. O'Hanlon, *Caste, Conflict and Ideology* (Cambridge, 1985). See her summary and analysis of Phule's play *Tritiya Ratna* ('Third Jewel'), p. 122.

12 *Collected Works of Mahatma Jotirao Phule* (in Marathi), (Bombay, 1991).

13 Madhusudan Dutt's letter to his friend Rajnarayan Bose, cited by Ghosh, op. cit., p. 138.

14 Warren Hastings, 'Letter to Nathaniel Smith' in P. J. Marshall, ed., *The British Discovery of Hinduism* (Cambridge, 1970), pp. 184–191.

15 Cited in Peter Gay, *The Bourgeois Experience* (Oxford, 1984), VOL. 1, p. 52.

16 See his five essays on the subject in *G. G. Agarkar Nibandha Sangraha* ('Collected Essays'; in Marathi) in M. D. Altekar, ed., *Sampurna Agarkar* ('Collected Works of Agarkar'; in Marathi), (Pune, 1940), VOL. 3, pp. 95–124.

17 Gay, op. cit., p. 32.

18 Ibid., p. 43.

19 Ibid., p. 60. Gay used the term 'renascent mysticism'. However in the translation edited by Steven Lukes (London, 1962), the words are 'resurgent mysticism'. See p. 33.

20 Cited in Dominik La Capra, *History and Criticism* (London, 1985), p. 125.

21 Ibid., p. 115.

22 *Rajwade Lekhasangraha* ('Selected Essays of V. K. Rajwade'; in Marathi), (New Delhi, 1967, second edition), pp. 266–77.

23 T. V. Sardesmukh, *Andhar Yatra* (in Marathi), (Bombay, n.d.). Sardesmukh certainly argues that the images of darkness were the high point in that poetry.

24 Rahul Sankrityayan, 'Bharatendu aur Pushkin' in *Rahul Sankrityayan ke Srestha Nibandh* (in Hindi), (New Delhi, 1982), pp. 124–129.

25 See Sukumar Sen, *History of Bengali Literature* (New Delhi, 1960), p. 191.

26 Ibid., p. 185.

27 Jambhekar's article welcoming the Hindu *nataksata* (drama company) appeared in *Darpana* on 17 February 1832. For the text of the article, see G. G. Jambhekar, ed., *Memoirs and Writings of Acharya Balsastri Jambhekar* (*1812–1846*), (Pune, 1950), VOL. 2, p. 27.

28 McGregor, *Hindi Literature*, p. 73.

29 P. G. Sahasrabuddhe, *Maharashtra Sanskriti* (Pune, 1979), p. 801.

30 Cited by McGregor, *Hindi Literature*, p. 68.

31 Ichalkaranjikar also started *Sangit Darpan* in 1883, a Marathi journal on music, perhaps the first in India.

32 Unfortunately, I was not able to locate any account which traces the history of the centres of production of musical instruments. It would be interesting to find out when Miraj, a small and dusty town at the southernmost tip of Maharashtra, started producing sitars. Peter Gay mentions (op. cit. p. 28) how, in 1884, the English periodical *Musical Opinion* reported that Germany (in that year) could boast of approximately 424 factories turning out about 73,000 pianos a year. It is a pity that such data was not available for new or old centres of production of musical instruments in India.

33 T. W. Adorno, *The Aesthetic Theory* (London, 1984), pp. 313, 314.

34 Amilcar Cabral: *Unité et Lutte* I, p. 44 in Patrick Chabal, *Amilcar Cabral: Revolutionary Leadership and People's War* (Cambridge, 1983), p. 183.

35 Cabral, ibid., p. 43, cited in Chabal, ibid.

36 Aimé Céssaire's interview with the Haitian poet Rene Depestre at the Cultural Congress of Havana, 1967 in *Aimé Céssaire: Discourse on Colonialism* (New York, 1972).

'The Kingdome of Darkness'
or The Problem of Culture

Close to half a century ago Maurice Dobb wrote an essay on 'capitalism' which has become quite a classic. The opening sentences of the essay read as follows:

> It is perhaps not altogether surprising that the term Capitalism . . . should have been used so variously, and that there should have been 'no common measure' of agreement in its use. What is more remarkable is that in economic theory, as this has been expounded by the traditional schools, the term should have appeared so rarely, if at all.[1]

Almost the same words can be used about *Bharatiya sanskriti* (Indian culture). The traditional schools of thought in India do not use the term at all. There was a famous book by Sane Guruji of the same name.[2] But even that book was more an attempt to refute the distortions of Hinduism and Indian culture that the Hindu nationalists were trying to popularize in the late 1930s and early 1940s. Thus the Hindu nationalist Savarkar's view of Indian culture and the view of a Gandhian like the late Sane were as different from each other as can be. Perhaps Savarkar does not offer the best comparative paradigm. There would be any number of Hindu nationalists who would have very little to do with Savarkar's world-view. Their favourite would be Vivekananda.[3] One can go on citing examples of this kind. The point is: what is *Bharatiya sanskriti* and, more particularly, what meaning and significance does one attribute to the term Hindu? Scarcely an easy question to answer. This is not to suggest that there is no such thing as Hinduism or Hindu. To be sure there is, except that it is not easy to describe, let alone define.

This is further complicated by the fact that in most Indian languages there does not exist a term for culture which predates the colonial period. Even the word *sanskriti* is a coinage and that too of a fairly recently vintage. In Bengali, the term *kristi* (like *bildung* in German) was popular for a while and, as discussed in an earlier essay, we learn from Suniti Kumar Chatterji's account that it was at Tagore's initiative that the term *sanskriti* was preferred and came to stay in Bangla as the standard word for culture. In many languages (Marathi, for example) no clear distinction is made between culture and civilization in terms of the use of separate words for both. More often than not, *sanskriti* serves the purpose and it is the context which makes it clear if culture or civilization is being referred to.

1

It is obvious that this does not and cannot mean that there was no culture. After all, even in English, the usage is not very old. The Oxford English Dictionary traces the word to 1483. But it was then employed to mean 'worship: reverential homage' and so on. The first major work in which the term culture in its modern sense is employed is Hobbes' *Leviathan* (1651). Hobbes talks of 'the education of children' being 'a culture of their minds'. This obviously comes from the Latin *cultura* which meant cultivation, tending, in Christian authors. Hobbes, however, takes the notion a few steps forward. The point is that culture as a secular category emerges even in Europe only in the seventeenth century. This has to be also understood in conjunction with Kantian and Hegelian thought. Kant, through his three critiques, made it easy to establish aesthetics and therefore culture as an autonomous category. On the other hand, with Hegel, as Marcuse has pointed out, '. . . history no longer remained a process confined to one region . . .'[4] To be sure, Marcuse is talking here of the regions of spirit and of nature (in his discussion of Dilthey's analysis of Hegel), but the statement is true also in a more primary sense inasmuch as with Hegel 'history' becomes a universal category going beyond regions. In short, with Hegel we have 'world history' for the first time. With Hegel, history emerges as a singular noun. 'History' takes the place of histories.

It would seem that the process of a growing consciousness of culture has taken a different, almost opposite, course. In precolonial times, as we have seen, culture as a term did not exist in most Indian languages. Everything was dharma. It has become a cliché in contemporary discussions that dharma is not religion. If we had precolonial India in view, it would be right to argue that dharma was inclusive of both 'ritualistic' or 'religious' and secular elements. Thus *yajana* and *yajana* (to perform rituals like *puja* and *yajna* and to officiate at these rituals as a priest) were the *dharma* of a brahman. But so were *adhyayana* and *adhyapana* (study and teaching). An actor had his *dharma* (so much so that in our times the terms karma and dharma have been reviled in the Indian-language discussions of theatre. A late nineteenth-century or early twentieth-century theatre hardly ever used these terms). This was no less true of the non-Hindus. Islam here had a distinct Indian character and it did not fight shy of accommodating elements from the other metaphysical or even secular traditions. This is particularly so in the fields of culture, more specifically in music, dance and literature.

Sometime in the nineteenth century the situation clearly starts changing. The pace and timing of change have varied in different parts of India. But its overall thrust has been unmistakable. To begin with, dharma began acquiring the characteristics of religion as the term is normally understood. The transformation is still not complete. But the signs of change are also clearly visible. 'Hinduism' not only emerges as a fairly definable category, it also gets semitized in the process. With or without their knowledge, our leading figures of the time try to turn the religious system of India into what could be described in Weberian terminology as 'rational', i.e. disciplined or organized religion. One sees this change coming across the board as it were. Indian Islam is increasingly projected as totally unrelated to the mass of 'Hindus' around it. It would not be very wrong to say that the Indian elite (both Hindu and Muslim) may shift from one civilization to two nationalities. The Indian Marxists used this terminology much later. But their erroneous use of this theory to understand the Hindu-Muslim problem demonstrated the divide that the elite was imposing upon itself over a century. The masses were dragged into it, continue being dragged into it. In backward societies (in particular) this is inevitable. But they did not quite share this perception. This is demonstrated by the poor response that the Hindu Mahasabha and the Muslim League as political parties generally evoked among the followers of the respective faiths. The masses suffered the elite desire to destroy their culture silently. Perhaps a better way of putting it is that they were reluctant victims of the politicization of their faiths by the elites, both Hindu and Muslim.

2

It is interesting to see the manner in which this politicization took place and the general cultural significance of that politicization. I will limit my comments to Hinduism because that is an area I know fairly well. But it would be a mistake to assume that the phenomenon being described here was limited to the Hindus alone. Colonialism and early Indology planted several myths in the Indian mind. One of them was the belief that Aryans and Dravidians were, in fact, races. The reality is that the terms can be conveniently used for classification of Indian languages. That a given group of languages presupposes a race speaking those languages has no scientific basis whatsoever. At any rate, whatever justification this belief might have had in the nineteenth century, today it has to be rejected as baseless and incorrect. There is no race called the Aryan race. This is also true of the so-called Dravidian race. There are Dravidian languages. There is a group of Indo-European languages.

But the myth persists. So some people argue that it is a hoax perpetrated by the Europeans about the Aryans coming to India from elsewhere. Some others equally strongly reject this 'revivalist' or 'chauvinistic' position. It would not be easy to cite another example of a debate over the origins of a non-existent phenomenon. In the last decades of the nineteenth and the early decades of the twentieth century, debate served the purpose of defining 'we' in terms of 'the other'. Very few people thought of whether the debate was legitimate at all. By now, however, it has got so totally confused that one does not know if the people of India would ever be able to get out of the clutches of the non-existent Aryan-

Dravidian divide. The reason why the myth persists or will persist is probably the fact that in a caste-society all categories of discrimination are easily accepted and legitimized.

The early Indological research fuelled this extraordinary race myth. European Romanticism, especially German Romanticism, created a view of an Aryan race and an Aryan India. In classical Sanskrit, the word *arya* is never used in the sense of race. But the myth persisted. Along with it was born the myth of a superior civilization of a superior people. All ancient civilizations have entertained the idea of superiority. It was true of the Greeks and Romans. It was also true of the Chinese. The difference, in the case of India, consisted in the fact that a colonized or rather vanquished people needed that myth not so much as a view of 'the other' but as one of the 'sources of the self'.[5] The ideas of and about India generated by European Romanticism became a major constituting element of the Indian personality. We live in times when, among the English-speaking liberals of India, at least an articulate section of them, the idea of India itself has probably become questionable. It is not easy, therefore, to see the force of these ideas or that the appeal of the idea of India exists rather strongly for the not-so-enlightened people of this country. Since the liberals have lost interest in it, other forces have emerged as the sole repository or exponent of the idea of India.

Let us return to the phenomenon of the nineteenth century alluded to above. It was a grand imitation project—imitation of alleged or real characteristics of the British who had subjugated us. It was thought that one of the secrets of their triumph was the organized, disciplined character of their faith. This was never quite articulated in these terms but if one looks closely at what was done to Hinduism in the nineteenth century, one can see this imitation vividly.

There are other reasons too. Let me illustrate the point in the context of western India. Catholicism had come to western India in the sixteenth century. But it had remained an exclusive sect with little or no interaction with the Hindus. There were conversions, of course, but the world of ideas of Hinduism was largely unaffected by them. The non-Catholic Christianity, which came to western India later, was not so passive. It began an active interaction with the Hindus and in the pages of *Dnyanodaya*, the Christian weekly originally published from Ahmednagar and later, from Bombay, there was a vigorous questioning of Hinduism, Hindu society and Hindu metaphysics. Not that all that was said was very meaningful. A lot of what it had to say was based on ignorance of the texts and prejudice. Nevertheless, it generated a debate among the liberal Hindus, making them take a fresh look at the state of (western Indian) Hindu society of the time. It also generated a peculiar, distant admiration for Christianity. Witness Jotiba Phule's famous play *Tritiya Ratna*.[6] His term for God—*nirmeek*—was a clear borrowing from the Christian tradition. So was the Indian trinity—the Sanskrit coinage of *Satyam Shivam Sundaram* (The Truth, the Auspicious and the Beautiful), to cite just one example from Bengal.[7]

The Prarthana Samaj was influenced by the Brahmo Samaj of Bengal, but both in turn were influenced by the Church. They started the practice of weekly prayer-congregations and even sermons. Paradoxically, all these imitations of Christianity and the rather brutal attacks on the Hindu way of life carried on by journals like *Dnyanodaya* stimulated the process of liberalization and reform in Hinduism. Without any conscious design or even a fleeting awareness of the consequences of the positions they were taking, the nineteenth-century (non-Catholic) Christians had contributed to a 'reformation' of a kind of Hinduism.

3

This 'reformation' had many aspects, but perhaps the most important was fashioning Hinduism after Christianity. The Christians had a book. The Hindus needed one. The *Bhagwad Gita* has always been an important text inasmuch as it was a part of the three main sources of Hindu metaphysics (along with the Upanishads and the *Brahma Sutras*; all three together known as *prasthanatrayi*: the three ways to salvation). But in the nineteenth century and, of course, well into the twentieth, the text of the *Gita* acquires a status of 'the Book', as the term is normally understood in the Semitic religions.

The Hindus had finally found their book. A number of nationalists like Bal Gangadhar Tilak, Aurobindo Ghosh, Vivekananda, Gandhi and even Vinoba Bhave have written commentaries on the *Gita*. This connection between the 'Hindu' texts and our nationalist leaders had been interpreted by many as an attempt to use 'Hindu' symbols and texts for nationalist mobilization. Tilak's attempt at launching a *sarvajanik* Ganeshotsav (public festival of Ganesha) has also been interpreted in similar terms. It would seem, however, that these were imitations of Christianity in terms of creating a book and creating a collective festival, like a carnival.[8] In other words, these attempts were more Christian than Hindu; at any rate more imitative than authentic 'Hindu' if the *dharma shastras* (sacred scriptures) are anything to go by.

This 'organization' of an open-minded and even disorganized Hindu system was bound to result in the emergence of a new view of Hinduism and, therefore, of culture. The Satyashodhak movement of Phule and the Prarthana Samaj of Ranade and Bhandarkar had gone back to the medieval Bhakti poetry for the sources of religion. The other went back to the brahmanical tradition. If the former represented a revolt, the latter stood for a restoration of the Vedic tradition. In the context of the nationalist struggle with its unmistakable anti-imperialist overtones, this restoration was not an undesirable thing in itself. To an extent it was inevitable.

Modern Indian historiography has looked at this phenomenon in Hindu and Muslim terms. The controversy over 'Vande Mataram' is the most glaring example. But, in the process, the aspect of imitation of Christianity and Europe has been practically ignored. Acharya Javadekar, a thinker in the Gandhian-Marxian mould, has touched upon the metaphysical constituent of the nationalism in Bengal. He called it *bangalcha adhyatmik rashtravad* in his brilliant book on modern India first published in the late forties.[9] In an earlier book (published in 1940), he had traced the notion of metaphysical nationalism (*adhyatmik rashtravad*) to Hegel.[10] It seems to me that all traditional historical analysis has failed to fully see the connections between European influence and the apparently metaphysical expression that anti-imperialism had inevitably found in the nineteeth and early twentieth centuries. This is the reason why Javdekar's writing is important. Unless one sees these connections it would not be possible to see continuities between Tilak and Vivekananda on the one side and Gandhi on the other and to explain why all of them had written commentaries on the *Gita.*

With the decline of anti-imperialism and now its disappearance, it is inevitable that a distorted view of nationalism and metaphysics should turn into revivalism. The forces which remained weak during the period of the nationalist movement have now come to dominate the scene. It was only a question of time before the metaphysical nationalism and religiosity turned into fundamentalism and revivalism which is what has happened. When the Indian state cannot and does not hold its own against the neo-colonialist onslaught, it creates a situation which is most appropriate to the talk of banning books, destroying places of worship like in Ayodhya and issuing fatwas to have people killed in the name of religion. Wilful destruction of the economy also results in wilful or otherwise destruction of culture. In a situation of crisis, an insurmountable one at that, it is not very difficult to understand that an average man may fear that but for his faith nothing else any longer belongs to him.[11] The professional community leaders then use this fear to usurp leadership and set into motion a process of lumpenization of politics, economy and culture.

4

In our situation, which does not obtain anywhere in the developing world, a unique phenomenon has been in operation. This phenomenon relates to the decline of Indian languages. Way back in the twentieth century, there was a movement to defend and advance the cause of Marathi in Maharashtra. Of course, this happened in other language areas too. The Bhakti movement gave voice to the lowly of the lowliest in our society, an authentic voice of self-expression. We are witness in present-day India to a situation of the near-planned eclipse of Indian languages. There was a time when the Indian elite was bilingual—deeply rooted in its linguistic tradition but also familiar with the modern European tradition.

Now a typical member of the elite is vaguely familiar with Europe but knows probably next to nothing about his language; the literary and the cultural are thrown out of the system because the system has no use for them. On the other hand, the people who manage culture are less and less familiar with what constitutes culture.

The net result is that culture acquires and indeed has acquired in our society a necessarily negative meaning. Society gets divided into 'we' and 'they'. So does culture. For a Hindu, being anti-Islamic becomes the only meaning of culture. It is the same with a Muslim. Our culture has also suffered from the language of pluralism and composite culture. As the French philosopher Gilles Deleuze has pointed out, pluralism is in the last analysis a variety of empiricism. And culture can never be understood in mere empirical terms. You cannot really take a view of Indian culture as pluralistic or composite without underlining the dividing line between the so-called Hindu and the so-called Muslim culture. There is an Indian culture—music and literature being good examples—which everyone shares and makes richer. What is Hindu or Muslim with the *raag-dari*? You cannot reduce Indian culture to empirical categories.

I am aware that 'plural' has been a necessary part of the secular discourse in our country. I submit that both empirical and deterministic approaches to Indian culture have been destructive. They have assumed that there is no plurality within Hinduism or within Indian Islam. Expressions like pluralistic tradition are a slightly sophisticated version of the slogan: *sarva dharma sama bhava* (equality among faiths and sects) which outlives its use if ever it was useful, just as Hindu metaphysics cannot be understood in terms of monotheism and polytheism. Indian culture cannot be understood in terms of a mono or plural tradition. At any rate, the talk of plurality has only encouraged the talk of uniformity or vice versa, if you will. Whereas plurality is a myth which the secular discourse does not wish to abandon, uniformity is a myth the revivalist and fundamentalist discourse does not wish to discard. The truth of the matter is that Indian culture is an organic and historically determined unity which has escaped us over a period of time almost simultaneously with the slow but hopefully not yet certain destruction of India.

It is not customary to hold the secularists responsible for this state of affairs. Political parties like the Bharatiya Janata Party, the RSS or the Vishwa Hindu Parishad talk of a pseudo-secularism. That argument need not be taken very seriously because any view which rejects a 'uniform' or atemporal and ahistorical (the word *sanatana* would mean that) view of Indian culture would be branded by them as pseudo-secular. The problem is not one of the correct use of the term: 'secular' was borrowed from the bourgeois philistines anyway. The point simply is to identify the cultural crisis of our time. Neither the category of plural or composite culture nor the category of uniform and *sanatana* culture would be very useful in identifying and facing that cultural crisis.

In other words, the Enlightenment project is still not over in our society. Neither the pre-modern categories (of Hindu and Muslim, etc.) nor the post-modern categories (of rejecting the grand-narratives or theories in favour of fragments) will help that project. The alternative to enlightenment is darkness. In this situation, the task of the liberals and the left becomes doubly urgent, for they alone can handle the problem of culture. Following Walter Benjamin they alone can emphasize that all histories of barbarism can give direction to the explorations in culture. It is for this reason that one has to identify the shortcomings of the secular discourse. I cited Hobbes at the beginning of this paper. It might be worthwhile to conclude with another citation from him. There is a section on 'The Kingdome of Darkness' in the *Leviathan* where he talks of forces very much comparable to what we have referred:

> . . . the Kingdome of Darkness . . . is nothing else but a Confederacy of Deceivers, that to obtain dominion over men in this present world . . .[12]

That is what we are witness to. The problem of culture is the problem of 'the Kingdome of Darkness' and of the 'Confederacy of Deceivers' who are out to destroy not only culture but society as well.

First published in Economic and Political Weekly, *16 July 1994*

Notes

1 Maurice Dobb, *Studies in the Development of Capitalism* (London, 1946).

2 P. S. Sane, popularly known as Sane Guruji, was a Gandhian thinker, nationalist leader and once a very popular novelist and poet in Marathi. The book that we allude to was also written in Marathi and was quite topical when it was first published in the forties inasmuch as it gave an alternative rendering of the Hindu world-view in polemical contrast to that of the Hindu nationalists.

3 This distinction is important because Savarkar had very little to do with Hindu metaphysics or theology. In contrast, for Vivekananda, nationalism became meaningful when and if it had *adhyatmik* (metaphysical) content in it. See also notes 7 and 8.

4 Herbert Marcuse, *Hegel's Ontology and the Theory of Historicity* (Cambridge, MA, 1987). See especially Chapter 26.

5 Charles Taylor, *Sources of the Self: Making a Modern Identity* (Cambridge, 1984). Taylor poses this problem mainly within the context of Western civilization. This short essay is an attempt at describing our modern identity and the way it was made.

6 Jotiba Phule (1827–90). A major social reformer who took the modernity debate in India to the shudras.

7 See note 9.

8 To be sure Tilak did not refer to the carnival at all. But his main point was that the people should have a communitarian festival which would give them a sense of unity, of belonging, going beyond caste and class. The carnival does that for the Christians and Tilak could not have been unaware of it. Yet I would agree that this is mere speculation, hopefully a plausible one.

9 Acharya Javdekar published a book in the late forties called *Adhunik Bharat* ('Modern India') which is a classic. This is the title of one of the chapters in the volume.

10 Acharya Javdekar. *Adhunik Rajyamimansa* ('Modern Theories of State', in Marathi), (Pune, 1940). This book also traced the European/Christian origins of the trinity of *Satyam Shivam Sundaram*.

11 I think Marx refers to the melancholy which colonialism provided in his India writings. But an even more relevant formulation would be that of the late Henri Lefebvre, the French Marxist. He says that under capitalism 'along with God, nature is dying.' See his *The Production of Space* (Oxford, 1991), p. 71. His description would apply to the Third World with even greater poignancy.

12 Thomas Hobbes, in his famous *Leviathan* (first published in 1651), has a section on 'The Kingdome of Darkness'. See pp. 331–384 of the Everyman's Library Edition (London, 1975).

The Ordinary and the Extraordinary in Creativity

1

You must all wonder what I am going to talk about. I am not sure if I know for certain. But then what does one do with certainty? I have no certainties to offer. More than a hundred years ago, Shaw once began a speech by saying that merely three words would be enough for the topic on which he was meant to speak: 'I don't know'. I find myself in a similar situation. What is ordinary and extraordinary in the creative? I don't know. That would be the right answer.

However, according to our tradition, such a position may not be the only one conceivable or possible. Consider the following from the *Kenopanishad*:

> *naham manye suvedeti, no na vedeti veda cha*
> *yo nastad veda tad veda no na vedeti veda cha*
>
> I do not think that I know it well, nor do I think that I do not know it. He who among us knows what is meant by this, knows. It is neither a state of not knowing, nor of knowing.

Or consider another verse from the same text:

> *yasyamatam tasya matam matam yasya na veda sah*
> *avijnatam vijnatatam vijnatamavijanatam*
>
> To whomsoever it is not known, to him it is known. To whomsoever it is known, he does not know. It is not specifically understood by those who specifically understand; it is specifically understood by those who do not specifically understand.

You can now see how much dialectic there is in this tradition. Those who celebrate it do not know about it. There could not have been a better forum than the Safdar Hashmi Memorial Lecture to remind them, and us, of that dialectic.

Anyway, to return to the peculiar relationship between 'specifically knowing' and 'not understanding', the position that Shaw took would probably not have been admitted as valid by our text which would have promptly posted a rejoinder: Shaw's disclaimer actually underlines the fact that he specifically understands (*vijnatam avijanatam*). And, indeed, Shaw did; for he went ahead and delivered a witty and entertaining address.

I cannot, of course, even pretend to match that wit and entertainment. Quoting Shaw, or an ancient Sanskrit text for that matter, is easy. One must, however, see beyond these. We have to remember that this business of knowing is itself dialectical, involving both the ordinary and the extraordinary. Both knowing and not knowing. Epistemology is as much about not knowing as knowing.

Further caveats are in order here. To begin with, I am discussing a problem of literary creativity. I am not discussing arts like music or painting. I am talking of *language.* All of our discussion today relates to and derives its legitimacy from the realm of the autonomy of the word. An obviously apocryphal but popular story about Sanskrit poet and playwright Kalidasa has it that Saraswati, Goddess of Learning, once asked him: *asti kaschit vagvilasah?* 'Do you have any excellence of speech?' (or, celebration of language, if you will). That encounter turned him into a poet and he produced three long poems. One began with *asti,* the other with *kaschit* and the third with *vag.* The ordinary Kalidasa became extraordinary. I refer to creativity in, and made possible within, language. There is complexity built into all creativity but it can be mind-boggling in language. Think of what Novalis said of Burke's writing on the French Revolution when it was published in 1790:

> . . . many anti-revolutionary books have been written in favour of the revolution. Burke, however, has written a revolutionary book against the revolution. (*Bluethenstaub* I)

I wonder if such a characterization of a musical concert would ever be possible. Probably not. It is possible in a literary discourse mainly because literary truth is always tendentious. In that tendentiousness it stands removed from concrete reality. Once, in a review of a Turkish novel I read a line from that novel:

> I do not want to be a tree for dogs to piss on . . . I want to be its meaning.

The tree wants to be its meaning; a concrete reality aspiring to be its abstraction. This is possible because meaning is never one. The word is a polyphonic phenomenon because it is tendentious. This tendentiousness forces you to rise from the abstract to the concrete provided, of course, you can or you wish to.

I speak of 'Indian languages'. I do not speak of Indians writing in English as recently celebrated and canonized in an elegant volume by Arvind Krishna Mehrotra. I refer to 'Indians Writing in English' in the way I presently will not because I have strong views on whether or not English is an Indian language; its status as an Indian or non-Indian language is not central to my argument. The relevant fact in terms of my argument is that most 'Indians Writing in English' write mainly for the Western, i.e. non-Indian market. Think, for instance, of the opening paragraph of *The God of Small Things* (*GOST*, which incidentally would come fairly close to the word in my language, Marathi, for a story—*goshth*—but let that pass). It begins with a description of the hot and humid May weather in Kerala. Had this novel been written in Malayalam or Marathi or Bangla, I wonder if it would have carried this information? Probably not. This description of May heat and the southwest monsoon could hardly have found a place in a desi or native novel; it would be so patently redundant. Heat and humidity are everyday facts and they would be narrated as such. In the case of *GOST*, its target-readership is unfamiliar with the weather and seasons of India. It certainly would know very little, if anything, about humid and sultry weather. Those who do not know heat, sweat and the monsoon must get the feel of it all. *GOST* has many snippets of such information. A case of good packaging. The target audience is happy because there are no clumsy and obscure details about distant lands and their too many people. I do not mean to suggest that all this happens because one writes in *English*. It happens because of the *market*. It is quite a commentary on this writing that *GOST* was described as an example of rich 'Indian writing'. You would rarely find a new or a first German or French or

English novel described as a rich *European* novel. But this target audience has little patience with the languages of India, as these 'Indians Writing in English' themselves do! They find this category of 'Indian' both good and convenient. It is almost a non-linguistic projection of the so-called India. Pure ethnicity in writing made possible by the new classical language of English! In Sanskrit plays, at least the classical and the native stood side by side. Here, the space of the native is what the 'ethnological' can permit.

Another example from the opposite end of the spectrum might help us understand this business of the 'ethnic'. If in *GOST* it was necessary to report weather conditions, in this other novel it was not necessary to do so. I refer to that absolutely delightful piece of writing, *White Teeth,* by Zadie Smith. The novel is 'set' in the migrant South Asian community in England (I know that Ms Zadie Smith is not an Indian) and it contains a Bangladeshi Muslim character who claims that Mangal Pande was his great grandfather. Now in a desi novel, such a mix-up of religious and caste identities would not happen. And if it were historically true, it would require an explanation, if not a subplot. In a typical *videsi* novel that may not be necessary because the demands of ethnicity have been adequately met; its market, or shall we say its preponderantly Anglo-American readership, would be quite happy with such details as are provided by an author who, they know, is not South Asian herself.

Friedrich Dürrenmatt, the famous Swiss playwright, once spoke of a distinction between *grosse macht* (great power) and *klein stadt* (small state) as making a difference to literary acceptance. What he did not account for was the *grosse markt* (great market). Ms Smith has only to provide some sounds which are ethnic enough and the 'extraordinary' effect is achieved. The 'extraordinary' curiosity kills the ordinary South Asian cat! The South Asian world is not an experiential world for this market. It better not be! It is the so-called 'rich Indian world', as *The Independent* described *GOST* once, already a near-continental description of a provincial reality. An 'ordinary' of a province is turned into an Orientalist extraordinary.

2

This business of English and desi has a direct bearing upon the 'creative' in India. The problem of English is *not* a problem of deciding whether or not English is or has become an Indian language. Rather, it is a problem of the classical and the vernacular. This is, of course, not only an Indian problem. Dante's *De Vulgaris Eloquentis* is widely regarded as the first work in Europe to assert the inherent superiority of the vital, vernacular languages over Latin. In an eloquent passage, Dante declares that that he will 'attempt to be of service to the speech of the common people [by] pouring into so great a vessel that water of my own wit'. In a sense, this passage would also explain Portuguese missionary Father Stephen's attempt to write a *Khrista Purana* (a long hagiographic poem on the life of Christ) in Marathi in the sixteenth century. The extraordinary in writing could be achieved, at any rate for Father Stephen, by writing in the vernacular. The Bhakti poets in medieval India likewise created the extraordinary by insisting on the ordinary word, the vernacular word. Eknath said:

> *Sanskrit bhasha deve keli*
> *Marathi kay chorapasoon zali?*
>
> Perhaps Sanskrit was created by the gods.
> But was Marathi made by thieves?

It was an extraordinary celebration of the ordinary, vernacular word. India has had three so-called 'classical' borders to deal with—borders between people, their speech and their cultural expression. First, there was Sanskrit. Then, there was Persian. Now, we have English. (One must add here that the protagonists of the so-called national language, Hindi, waiting in the wings to take the place of English, are hoping that their day of triumph is not far off after all!) The vernacular of England has become the classical language of India. Even Macaulay would not ever have dreamt of this situation! *Brahmanavada* (brahmanism) has been the only clear ideology of the creative. It privileged the classical against the desi—the native, or the vernacular if you will—in the creative. The insistence on the classical helped *brahmanavada* to keep what the great Sanskrit critic Vishwanatha has called *mahavakya* (literally, 'great utterance') away from the people. The Bhakti poets therefore asserted the vernacular. Their position may be described as follows: Yes, all our creativity is ordinary. It better be. Only thus can it be extraordinary. Sanskrit, Persian and now English impose upon our creative world a divide—a divide between the ordinary, i.e. the vernacular, and the classical, which insists on being treated as extraordinary. It was not for no reason that Tukaram proclaimed: 'Just as well that I am a shudra, otherwise I would have been crushed under the weight of my own ego!' The *brahmanavada* approach still persists in India and denies the linguistic and therefore the experiential plurality of the Indian people. The classical is unaware of the details, as it were. From its perspective, there is no such thing as a Marathi or Telugu or Tamil world. There is an undifferentiated 'Indian' world. We found *The Independent's* reception of *GOST* cited earlier both amusing and a little frightening for that very reason. Anyway, to return to Bhakti. A great phase of creativity was with us during those years (I refer to the medieval period in general). In the case of Marathi, roughly from the twelfth to the seventeenth centuries, the ordinary, i.e. the vernacular, was celebrated. *Brahmanavada* stands for the extraordinary and the classical. Bhakti stood for the ordinary and the vernacular.

No, this *not* an argument against Sanskrit—or English for that matter. The argument is rather for a degree of scepticism about the 'brahmanical' and the 'classical' in aesthetics. In one sense, it is to argue that 'aesthetics' is an ideological category. Perhaps for that reason it greatly internalized the quality of the literary (*sahitya*) to the text or the words. (This might explain some post-structuralist enthusiasm for the categories of ancient aesthetics. Think of Todorov's discussion of categories such as *abhidha, lakshana, vyanjana* and so on). The need of the classical that our elite so strongly feels today is not classicism but a desire to 'package' the so-called 'Indian literature'. It may be mentioned here *en passant* that the term 'elite' actually meant a commodity in the seventeenth century. Bottomore cites the authority of Edmund Huguet to say that in the sixteenth century 'faire elite meant to make a choice (of merchandise)'. Our elite too make a choice, a choice of a classical or an extraordinary language which gives them access to the world market as part of a commodity of the 'other world'. Third World languages and literature then become the 'other'. The choice of language for literary expression is thus a political act. It makes the market—a hard currency market at that—a decisive part of the creative process and, of course, the languages which indisputably belong to that market. To be sure, this phenomenon is not altogether new to this country. In ancient times, in a sense, Sanskrit played a similar role. The Delhi court had conferred a similar status on Persian. And there are any number of people in this country who hope that one day Hindi will achieve the same status. There were powerful voices of protest and rebellion each time. If Dante saw the vitality of the vernacular in contrast to Latin, poets like Dnyaneshwar or Tukaram claimed the same vitality and power for Indian vernaculars. The difference today is perhaps that the celebration of the vernacular is now far more hopeless than it ever was. This may be indicative of the several battles that the coloured people of the world are losing. But we shall let that pass.

The medieval period of our history, roughly from the twelfth to the eighteenth centuries, was very creative because of the dialectic between the imposed classical language and the vital *lokabhasha* (people's language). The point is that our discussion must be, and indeed is, a little distant from Sanskrit, the erstwhile classical language, or English, which is decidedly taking over that field. It is easy to keep Sanskrit at a distance because there is no market involved. With English it is a different story. I am not suggesting a boycott of Sanskrit or anything like that. We must study that language but primarily to quote from it! There is no escape from owning and appreciating the classical but that does not mean that one has to live only in its world.

Let me say what must appear to many a preposterous thing. We must say that we are not very ancient people. Most of us begin our history sometime at the beginning of the second millenium. We have an ancient past. But our medieval past is where, linguistically, we have to locate ourselves. This does not and need not mean that we deny Sanskrit (or Persian, or English, or Hindi/Urdu). All that it means is that we assert our ordinary beginnings so that the extraordinary in creativity can be retrieved or attained. Tukaram once said:

> [Marathi] words are the only
> Jewels I possess
> Words are the only clothes I wear
> Words are the only food
> That sustains my life
> Words are the only wealth
> I distribute among people
> Says Tuka
> Witness the word
> He is God
> I worship Him
> With words.

(Translation by Dilip Chitre. The first word in the first line [Marathi] is my addition.)

The extraordinary thing in this creativity was the status accorded to and allowed for the vernacular. This movement made the triumph of the (vernacular) word possible. The word became social in the truest sense because it was the word of the people.

Establishing and arguing for the 'contradiction' between the classical and the vernacular is not to pose a relationship of irreconcilable opposition between the two. I am *not* arguing against any language or any writing, not even Indo-Anglian writing. The question is whether the market determines what and how you write and whether that market is essentially made of the people the writing in fact portrays. In short, what contradictions are inherent in any given writing process. I am not interested in pure oppositions in literature. They do not exist. Or if they do, they do so in bad literature.

3

Tradition has posed the problem of what I have chosen to call ordinary and extraordinary in the following terms. The term *sahitya* (the term for literature in Sanskrit and most Indian languages) was explained as *shabda* (the word) and artha (*meaning*) being *saha* (together). When word and meaning go together, this (or their *sahabhava,* being together) produces *sahitya* or literature. But again, as the great Sanskrit critic Kuntaka pointed out:

> *shabdarthau sahitaveta pratitau sphuratah sada*
> *sahitaviti taneva kimapurvam vidhiyate*
>
> There is a *sahabhava* of *shabda* and *artha* in everyday speech. What then is extraordinary in the *sahabhava* in *sahitya*?
>
> (*Vaktroktijivita,* 1/16)

Kuntaka's question should not be interpreted to mean that *sahabhava* is not a relevant answer to the question, 'What is literature?' He would readily grant its relevance. His argument could possibly be that the central question relates to the special feature (*apurvam*) of this *sahabhava* in literature: *kim apurvam vidhiyate.* He argues that *sahabhava* is made *apurva* by the *yogyata, akanksha* and *sannidhya* of the *padas* (words). This means that words should deserve (*yogyata*) to be together. They should aim (*akanksha*) at being together. They should actually (*sannidhya*) be together. This threefold *sahabhava* results in a *vakya* (an utterance, by extension a literary expression) and a bunch of such *vakyas* is a *mahavakya.* Kalidasa's *Raghuvamsha* would be such a *mahavakya.*

I am going to talk a lot about and from Sanskrit. I have to, because the most crucial question of literature was posed in that language. More precisely, the central question of literature changed from one formulation into another. Before Kuntaka, the major critic of the early medieval period, the standard question was: 'What is *alankara*?' or 'What is the device of beauty in literature?' (*Alankara* is, literally, 'figure of speech'). Kuntaka changed all that. He raised the question, the right and relevant question, *Kim etat sahityam*? 'What is literature?'—he asked. It seems to me that he shifted the focus from formalistic aesthetics to the essential question of literary criticism. Criticism must ponder the question 'What constitutes literature?' or, to put it alternatively, 'What should be inherent in a given piece of writing in order to qualify as literature?'

Now it is indisputable that Sanskrit discourse on literature goes back to ancient times. You may push it back as much as you like. It has a long history. Against that background I find it fascinating indeed that an early *medieval* critic raises a central question of criticism and almost liberates that discourse from formalistic aesthetics. In a sense, therefore, criticism and perhaps also history —criticism and history relevant to *us*, that is—begins then, roughly around the eighth or ninth century AD that is, the time that vernaculars appear on the scene (with the exception of Tamil and Kannada, which are older). It is perhaps not entirely a coincidence that the first vernacular sentences are formulated at the same time as the crucial critical question is raised in Sanskrit poetics, *kim etat sahityam*?

This shift inevitably brought about an almost a two-camp divide among critics, in conjunction with the linguistic divide between the classical and the vernacular. The French critic Jean Paulhan has divided theorists into two groups: the rhetoricians and the terrorists! We may use his classification thus: those who did not go beyond *alankara* or *reeti* were rhetoricians. All students of literary theory in India would be familiar with terms like *reeti*, *shabdalankar* and *arthalankara* and would not need any elaboration or comment. Students of literary theory must learn these terms and what they mean. But one cannot avoid the impression that they are a bit like brahmanical rituals: interesting, but not, in the end, quite necessary. I would not argue that they add nothing to a piece of literary writing. They do. Nevertheless they do not give you the essence of literature.

Therefore the 'terrorist' has to question their utility or, more accurately, their claims to centrality to the literary discourse in much the same way as the Bauddhas or Charvakas questioned the doctrine of *atman*. Brahmanical literary science needed the 'terrorists'. It had come to be more or less 'Ancient Indian Formalism' much like Russian Formalism—with the difference that the latter was a living school. Medieval India needed to ask that question, 'What is literature?'

I do not mean to suggest that formalism by its very nature needs to be rejected. That would be patently wrong. It is like rejecting melodrama. You may or may not like it but there is no gainsaying the fact that it is a legitimate form of art. In a like manner, formalism is also a legitimate form of criticism but there is a need to move away from it. The 'terrorists' of early medieval India were doing precisely that. They questioned the brahmanical tradition which may have been quite creative at one stage but had ceased to be so at another. There was, however, always the 'terrorist' tradition represented by the *avaidik darshanas*—Bauddha, Jain, Charvaka and similar traditions, which had sought to go beyond the formalism of the 'rhetoricians'.

There is a Buddhist text called *Saddharmachintamani* which discusses the method of sculpting a statue of the Buddha. The text's advice is interesting and perceptive. It says that the sculptor should look at the (presumably already existing) Buddha sculpture, think of its *pramana* (the proportions and the standard) and *tad dhyatva bhittau niveshayat*: contemplate the *pramana* and then transfer that thought into his creation. Whatever a sculptor or a painter thinks of the Buddha, he has to transfer that thinking into his creative process. It is thus very different from creating an *alankara*. It is a movement away from naturalism and to realism properly understood. When a sculptor or a painter transfers his understanding or his perception which his contemplation of reality (in this case, the form of the Buddha) endows him with into his sculpture or mural, he succeeds in creating a work of art. In other words, *sahitya* does not describe what is but the author's intellectual, or creative, if you will, *intervention* in what is. Creativity thus is an interventionist process.

Therefore, what is ordinary and extraordinary would depend upon what kind of *dhyana* (thinking) has gone into that intervention and what it has done of the *pramana*. It can even be a revolutionary intervention against the revolution, in the manner of Burke, as Novalis pointed out. Such are the paradoxes and the dialectics of the situation we are talking about. Raymond Williams famously asserted that culture is ordinary. One may extend that argument. Even creativity at one level is ordinary. But then, even life is ordinary. I live an ordinary life. The word is also ordinary. I think over this ordinariness (*dhyatva*) and thereby transform that life, that word, into something extraordinary. There is a further caveat to this proposition in terms of the dynamics of the ordinary and extraordinary: the moment the author becomes conscious of the 'extraordinary', his word becomes ordinary again.

This process can occur at the level of reading as well. The reading of a text and its centrality need not be dismissed as a post-modernist or post-structuralist fancy. In the classical Indian tradition, a play has been described as *anantapatha* which means that it is capable of being read in several (literally, endless) ways. The text thus multiplies itself almost eternally. A classicist would perhaps make it a condition of extraordinariness. I have always felt that a playwright writes dead words. They come alive—at times in contradiction with the playwright's intentions—when someone reads or visualizes or enacts them. The written word has its cycle of life and death, a thesis of reincarnation (*punarjanma*), almost. It is ordinary when it is dead. When it comes alive, it becomes extraordinary. All culture is ordinary but in the social acts of looking at it, it transforms itself into the extraordinary. The source of extraordinariness in this reasoning is located in social reception, a typical 'terrorist' act, you might say!

I mentioned the story of how Kalidasa was asked if he had any *vagvilasa* to show. No Buddhist theoretician of literature would ever entertain that question, I imagine. The point I am trying to make is that the argument of extraordinariness is not author-oriented at all. It is not a *pratibha jnana* (ability or knowledge acquired by intuition or inspiration). The Kalidasa story is so typical of the brahmanical aesthetics which makes the creative act into an almost divine act. I think in order to understand this business of creativity it is far more useful to be aware of the fact that when I create I am not being divine. Rather, I am being completely human.

There is only one possible relationship with divinity that an author can and perhaps does establish. It lies in silence. Flaubert said somewhere that a novelist should never speak in the novel because the novelist is God and God never speaks! So, possible divinity lies in authorial silence! Anyway, we have the same relationship between speech and silence, between knowing and not knowing, between withdrawal and intervention; in other words, between ordinary and extraordinary.

Let us return to the classical Sanskrit critic Vishwanath and his term *mahavakya* (great utterance) for literature. We may understand his term thus. There is a *mahavakya* like the story of Shiva. From this larger text Kalidasa produced *Kumarsambhavam*, which is a smaller text. One may see a similar relationship between his *Raghuvamsha* and the *mahavakya* of the Ramayana. There is thus a movement from a larger text to a smaller text. In the Bhakti tradition, in contrast, there is a movement from a smaller to a larger text. The *Gita* is a small text. The *Dnyaneshwari*, a commentary on it in poetry, is a larger text. Tukaram wrote several thousand poems—according to Vamana Pandit, this was the clearest (*shuddha*, as he called it) statement of the Vedanta, again a movement from a smaller text to a larger one.

The Bhakti tradition celebrated these larger texts. The ordinary masses of Maharashtra do not read the *Purva Mimansa*, the Upanishads, the *Gita*, or texts like that. They read Tukaram or Dnyaneshwar. It would not be difficult to cite examples of the alternative larger texts that medieval India produced. In the classical or Sanskrit philosophical tradition the Upanishads, the *Brahma Sutras* and the *Gita* are taken to be the crucial texts, the *prasthanatrayi* as they are called. The mass movement of Bhakti in medieval Maharashtra created its own *prasthanatrayi* consisting of the *Dnyaneshwari*, Eknath's commentary on the eleventh chapter of the *Bhagavat Purana* as its own *prasthanatrayi*. The movement from the small to the large was thus canonized. It is also a movement from the ordinary to the extraordinary. The Vedanta was dead for the people. Tukaram brought it to life and changed it in the process.

This transformation from the ordinary to the extraordinary has been going on for many centuries. This business of turning the extraordinary (Sanskrit) texts into ordinary texts must have gone on for a long enough period for it to worry the defenders of the brahmanical tradition. Indeed, a medieval brahman pandit decided to hit back in terms of the small text which he wanted to prevail. Vamana Pandit, a seventeenth-century poet, has done a translation of the *Gita*. In the second chapter of the *Gita* there is a description of the *atman*, the immutable soul:

> *Na yenam vetti hantaram yashchainam manyate hatam*
> *Ubhau tau na vijanito nayam hanti na hanyate*

One thinks that the *atman* kills, another thinks that it cannot be killed. Both views are incorrect. It is interesting that the original verse does not attribute these erroneous views to anyone in particular. Vamana Pandit, however, in what purports to be a *translation*, attributes them to the Charvakas and those whom he calls *bhedavadi* or 'split-tists'. It is clear that the original Sanskrit does not even mention the words that the pandit employs in his translation. In other words, the pandit was doing an interventionist translation; except that this intervention was in favour of the established order. The problem of the ordinary and the extraordinary is located in the intervention. That is why Dnyaneshwar's commentary on the *Gita* is extraordinary in contrast to the ordinary of the pandit's translation.

We must also remember that such interventionist writing or this tendency of turning literature into a battleground could happen only in the vernaculars. Unlike the 'classical' languages, they have no choice but to be drawn into the battleground of the ordinary and the extraordinary. This did not and need not happen in a classical language because it does not speak in anybody's experiential world. It speaks in the language of the market as today's classical language does; or it speaks in the language of metaphysics, which has little real relationship with people's lives. This is the reason the medieval Bhakti tradition rejected the extraordinary of the classical, brahmanical tradition, and adopted the ordinary of the *avaidik* and the vernacular. In the process, it turned the categories of the ordinary and the extraordinary on their heads and showed, yet again, how symbiotically these categories are linked to the people and the vernaculars.

The Tenth Safdar Hashmi Memorial Lecture, New Delhi, 2001

Yesterday we had an interesting discussion on an experiment in theatre which sought to build a discourse of change and transformation through theatre. It is not my purpose either to discuss or to react to that experiment or even to react to a fascinating idea of turning the audiences into creative participants in a play. I refer to it mainly to share a peculiar uneasiness with you. It seemed to me that the experimentation was permeated with a degree of revolutionary romanticism which is far removed from whatever I have to say. I find such revolutionary optimism, the optimism that the theatre changes its spectators, to be increasingly unwarranted and in a fundamental way, a kind of an optical illusion. It seems almost to say: 'Look, we did a play, and the world has changed! At any rate, now that the audiences have created their own text, the first steps towards the transformation of the world have been taken.' At times I get the feeling that the world probably changes but India does not, in a manner of speaking. The situation is of a kind where there is, in reality, no discourse of tolerance, let alone of transformation.

Chairman Sadanand Menon referred to Kalidasa's play, *Vikramorvashiyam* in his opening remarks. Allow me to refer to the very first dialogue in that play which opens with the leading lady Urvashi and her friends being pursued by the *rakshasas*. The frightened heroine and her friends cry out for help thus:

> *Paritrayatam paritrayatam yassurapakshapati yasya va ambaratalegatirasti*
>
> Oh Lord, save us. Save us. Is there anyone who is the protagonist of the gods and who can fly into the skies? Oh, save us!

India is in the same state as Urvashi. Its battlecry ought to be the same. *Paritrayatam, paritrayatam*! We are in the midst of a social crisis. It is well said that theatre is always in crisis. I do not, however, mean to speak of that perennial crisis. I mean instead to speak of the social crisis and the impossibility of the cultural situation. I mean to speak of the crisis of tolerance in our midst.

Let me add a small caveat here. We live in difficult times. There is a plethora of incidents, more or less violent, that are happening around us almost without pause. But I do not intend to list them or to analyse them because those incidents by themselves do not really tell us anything new. The first or the one hundred and seventy-fifth tells you essentially the same story. The tragic part of it all is that it has been happening all the time or so it would appear.

Consider the following story in the *Natyashastra*, the classic handbook of performing arts in Sanskrit. The *suras* (the gods) and the *asuras* (demons) were watching a play together. The play seems to have evoked a contradictory and strong reception, resulting in violence between those who liked the play and those who did not. The violence spread in all directions, out of the empty space of performance. The story has it that this incident led to the construction of the first auditorium, presumably because some people thought that it might be safer to play in a more defined and controllable space. As you can see, things have not changed much since times immemorial.

Or consider the following. The same classic recommends that India is the land where theatre should be done. The reason it gives is because there is so much of *duhkha* (sorrow or suffering) in India. It is the suffering and violence which make theatre so eminently doable in this country. The story I narrated to begin with tells us how difficult, if not impossible, it is to do theatre. What does this mean, then? It means that anybody who wishes to do meaningful theatre here in our land wants to do the impossible. Imagine the crisis that is involved in doing meaningful theatre. Doing theatre is to discover that it is a creation of one's own world in a situation of no tolerance. It is trying to create a little meaning within a hostile world.

That word 'tolerance' is crucial. How far can one take it? In Europe, it does not go beyond the Enlightenment. Most Indian languages use the term *sahishnuta* or *sarvadharmasamabhava.* Traditionally, the former term was not limited to tolerance between faiths as the English term tolerance or the German term *duldung* has been. It was a broader term which included in its fold a certain awareness and respect for a plurality of views. Even so, it is not clear how far back in history one can actually take this term. My own guess is that it does not go beyond the colonial period. This is probably because tolerance or coexistence of faiths or religions became a problem in any significant way only during that time. The new colonial system had very little use for *sahishnuta.* On the contrary, it seemed to benefit from the increasing strife and distrust between faiths. This was the reason that the colonial ethos did not even pose the question that Kant had, about the 'subjective nature' of doctrinal faith. The colonial authorities who had otherwise thought of a whole range of ideas of and for the Indian people left the concept of tolerance out of their schema.

This is, however, not to suggest that there were no problems about terms like tolerance or sufferance during early Enlightenment. Indeed, Kant himself had at one place talked of the *hochmuetigen* (arrogant) name of *toleranz* (toleration). In any event these terms were a product of contemporary Europe's need to practise *duldung* between faiths. As such, the term tolerance carries with it a certain culture of peaceful coexistence of faiths. It is therefore important not to be carried away by what Kant described as the arrogance of the term as the moderns or post-moderns amongst us could so easily do.

The other term is the contribution of Gandhian thought. An eighteenth-century German lexicon put its finger on what the term tolerance meant or was intended to mean. It said that 'this word is as a whole used by an authority that allows other religious groups outside of the established religion'. In eighteenth-century Europe, tolerance was essentially thought of in terms of the relationship between a dominant Christianity and defensive Judaism. (No wonder Kant found the idea arrogant!)

Gandhi could hardly have adopted such a notion even if he were familiar with the Enlightenment thinking on the subject. He therefore chose a different path. He postulated a certain abstract religiosity, the intensity of which was what mattered. The source of this approach was not Sanskrit tradition. It was located more in the Prakrit or, more specifically, in the Bhakti tradition which placed the relationship with God above everything else. It did not matter whether you were Hindu or Muslim or *savarna* or *avarna*. The religiosity or the relationship with one's own God is all-important.

The seventeenth-century Marathi poet Sali Muhammad says in one of his poems:

> *amhi zatiche brahman, amuche soyare musalman.*
>
> (I am a brahman by birth, my relations Muslims.)

A Muslim poet claiming to be a brahman! Today, the Hindus would not accept this line as legitimate poetry, let alone as an expression of intense religiosity which makes such transcendence possible. Fundamentalist Islamists would not accept it either. From their perspective it is outright *kufr* (blasphemy); he is a *kafir* (heretic), they would argue. Nobody seemed to mind his position then. His religiosity, its purity and intensity, made him everybody's kin as it were. Many poets produced great literature because of their all-encompassing religiosity. It is not a question only of the medieval. Over a period of time we seem to have lost our taste for such intensely plural religiosity. Gandhi affirmed its relevance and centrality. Nevertheless, the crucial question is what has happened to our world of ideas. We have to address ourselves to this question.

How does one do it? Our present crisis, the crisis in theatre, has two different aspects related to each other. One is a sort of fire-fighting which is, of course, necessary. We can do that (organizing demonstrations, signing statements and so on) either when a political group or a group like Habib Tanvir's Naya Theatre is being harassed as they were the other day when they tried to reproduce a traditional play *Ponga Pandit* in Madhya Pradesh. I have seen the play which is a pleasant farce on the stupidities and absurdities of the *brahmanvadi* system. There is no earth-shaking social criticism there. It is a *prahasana* (farce)—nothing more, nothing less. A Hindu nationalist can legitimately take pride in the fact that his tradition admits an attack on one of the fundamentals of the system. Then where was the problem? It is quite clear that the problem lay in the fact that the group concerned is associated with a Muslim artist. How can he preside over the critique of 'our' system? That was what the anger was all about.

Or think of the iconic *Ghashiram Kotwal.* Tendulkar's and Marathi theatre's international reputation has been established by this play. All of you have heard of it, if not actually seen it. Indeed, who has not? I have even acted in it! The play came under attack by the Pune brahmans because, in their view, it sought to malign Nana Phadnavis (d. 1810), Prime Minister of the Peshwa Court in Pune in the late eighteenth century. This play belongs to 1971–72 or thereabouts. The whole episode is just incomprehensible. There is an auditorium in Pune, the management of which still does not permit a show of the play, a good three decades after the play first went on stage.

The extraordinary thing about the whole business is that there was a play by Khadilkar who is celebrated as a Natyacharya (royal bard). He wrote a play nearly eighty years earlier, in 1891 if my memory does not fail me, which was not very complimentary to the Prime Minister of the Peshwas. Tendulkar's aspersions, if they could be called such, are quite mild in comparison. There is no explanation of the new culture of intolerance. Or perhaps there is.

Along with the decline of tolerance, there is also the decline of the word in theatre. It is probably the case that our elite has very little use for modernity and as such for the modern word. It suffers theatre in the age of the commercial cinema and, as in the commercial cinema, it has no use for the signifying word. Do theatre by all means, our elite seems to tell our performers. Jump around, beat drums if you will. An invitation to present the exotic ethnic stuff in some European capital will always be there. But do not turn to the word, the modern word. A whole range of ideas of modernity has been systematically shown the door over the years.

I think that we have to look a little closely at the fundamental difference between the reception to *Sawai Madhavrao Yancha Mrutyu* (the title of the Khadilkar play that I referred to earlier) on the one hand and to *Ghashiram* on the other. What has happened over a period of less than a century?

The big Enlightenment project that the period of colonialism had brought to the Asiatic lands and especially to India has been abandoned. One of the major features of that project was an extremely critical Hindu reformist movement which was spearheaded by people who were willing to stand up, and indeed did, to carry out a critical project on Hinduism. They verily built a movement of *atmashuddhi*, to use a typical Gandhian word. This movement was an all-India phenomenon. They were a group of people who were perfectly willing to be almost ruthlessly critical of their own faith. Somewhere along the line the project was abandoned. And, in contrast, the orthodoxy decided to push its own project. (It would not be entirely correct to describe them as the orthodoxy. In one very significant sense they had very little use for any 'fundamentalism'.) The orthodox project was not fundamentalist because it did not mean to be. It was meant to turn 'Hindu' into a political category. Everywhere else in the developing world the primordial consolidation took place on a theological or clerical basis. Here, among the Hindus, it is being organized on a secular basis; secular communalism of sorts, if you will! In this situation, the first thing that happens is that plurality and generosity of the tradition is denied. In the *Nyaya Sutras*, especially in Vatsyayana's commentary on it, the right to interpret the text has been given also to the *mlechchhas*, i.e. those considered to be outside of the system by the *brahmanvadi* system. At some stage this right was denied to them.

How does the average individual get to know that the right to interpretation of Sanskrit texts was once not an exclusive privilege of the brahmans? A Brechtian answer would have been: go and write a *lehrstuck* about it because that is one of the primary problems of your liberation movement. But none of the Brecht enthusiasts of our country wrote such a piece of didactic theatre.

Let me make a point about 'Indian Brecht' at this juncture. It also relates to the giving up of the Enlightenment project. It would seem that in much the same manner as Engels' *Anti-Duehring* it was time to write an *Anti-Brecht*! Our approach to Brecht is yet another example of giving up the Enlightenment project. It appears as if we had gone to Brecht for the wrong reasons. I have known something of Brecht in several Indian languages to make such a by no means surprising overstatement. Most people who did Brecht in this country depoliticized him. Why ? They could afford to. There is that famous book, *Postmodern Brecht*. We in our country conceived (and, of course, did) a post-political Brecht!

Think of the time when it happens. This happens at a time when we are through with three plans of development. The middle classes are now a reasonably well-to-do people, especially in our metros. The business of our brahmanical middle classes is to complain. So they will and they do! Yet it does not detract from the fact that this class saw a prosperity and well-being which it had not known in its entire history. Suddenly it found itself searching and looking for its 'roots'. As somebody has said, only trees have roots and trees are rather stagnant! The point I am trying to make is that these classes now became harbingers, definers and celebraters of 'roots'; some of them discovered that the search for roots would acquire an international veneer through Brecht. Make merry while Brecht lasts. And indeed, he did not last for a long time. Nobody does any Brecht any longer. He is the subject of seminars and nostalgic trips for some old-fashioned leftists. Anyway, there is no Brecht happening. In a sense, the social need of these middle classes turned Brecht into a neo-nationalist instrument. It was not his fault. It was the fault of those who played Brecht. Perhaps it was their socio-historical need to so depoliticize Brecht.

Without our knowing it, we started building a neo-nationalism, a cultural nationalism of sorts. We are paying the price for all of that. The crisis of theatre is not only created by the politicians and the political situation, but also by the theatre people themselves. I have dwelt on this subject in my earlier writing so I will not elaborate on it except to reiterate that the search for the so-called 'Indian theatre' is also part of the same phenomenon. There was an Austrian Indologist who once made a distinction between Hinduism, neo-Hinduism and pop-Hinduism. In much the same manner there was Brecht, neo-Brecht and, finally, pop-Brecht.

This business of roots has got to be looked into. Look at it this way. I live in Delhi. I occasionally visit Mumbai or Pune. In short, I am an urban man. I want a modern theatre of modern man's problems but, very often, especially in the festivals, I am given a package of Sanskrit drama, a variety of folk forms and, of course, depoliticized Brecht. The result is a split. While I enjoy one kind of theatre, I pretend to be proud of another kind. This is the theatrical avatar of a split personality. This is happening all over. And in all discourses. I can see the split around me. I do not see the split within me. That is the average Indian dilemma. This business of Hindu identity is also a part of this split personality. Let me cite the example of a fellow Maharashtrian, Savarkar. He proclaimed in 1923 that he did not accept the three main sacred sources of Hinduism—the Vedas, the Smritis and the Puranas. He debunked them in the name of Hindutva. He insisted that there was nothing theological about his Hindutva: the first theoretician of secular communalism, if you will.

There is such a thing as reluctance to join debate. A thick volume was published in 1951 called *Mahabharatavaril Vyakhyane—Lectures on the Mahabharata* by Balshastri Hardas. Some of you who occasionally dare to read Indian languages, especially Marathi, should take a look at it. Somewhere in the middle of it is a reference to Comrade Dange. Now what was Dange doing in the chapter on Draupadi or Karna, you must wonder. Though there is absolutely no reason for him to be present, nevertheless he is. Dange's book on ancient Indian history has been viciously attacked. This happened in 1951. A vicious attack of three pages on Dange in that book argues how communists do not understand history, how communists do not understand myths, Dange being the sterling example of that. Poor Dange! The communists do not mention him and the others malign him. Now at that point, in

1951, nobody defends Dange. At least, I have not seen anybody do so. After all, Balshastri Hardas was no ordinary fellow. What is Balshastri Hardas's importance? I would say, if that book was not written in 1951, so many *karsevaks* would not have gone from Maharashtra. Of course, it is an overstatement but a legitimate one. The whole point is these people understood that there is such a thing as a cultural battle. And they knew who to fight it with. Why Dange? Because at that point of time Dange was easily the most popular Maharashtrian communist. So they had to attack him. The man had vision, the man had wit. The point I am trying to make is not why Dange was attacked; the point simply is, that you do not take a historicized view of people like Dange or, more generally, the leaders of the Enlightenment project.

Let me cite another example of reluctance to fight a cultural battle wholeheartedly. Think of the IPTA: the IPTA was active in Mumbai in the late forties and early fifties. Good, bad or indifferent, there was a theatre tradition in Maharashtra. But there is no IPTA intervention in Marathi theatre of any significance. Why did it not happen? Why did nobody ask this question? In any case, we did not and, in the process, we surrendered a certain hegemony in this living theatre tradition which was more than possible. This hegemony is being exercised by you-know-who. I am not saying that all those who run successful theatre in Maharashtra are members of the Sangh Parivar. Of course they are not. But at a cultural level you don't require memberships. You are operating within a public social consciousness. In a sense, you become a vehicle of it. My submission is that although we forgot what we were a vehicle of, they never did. And that is the societal crisis.

Let me now move away from Maharashtra to give you one last example. There is a periodical which comes out from Gorakhpur called *Kalyan*. It was first published in 1952. There is a special number on Hindu Dharma. Now it has been reissued in a hardcover edition for fifty or sixty rupees. I picked it up at a railway station somewhere. The beautiful thing about that volume is its ignorance of Hinduism. After all, I am a born Hindu, and I don't disown the fact that fact. You know, there was a contemporary of

Goethe's who in his discussion of tolerance calls it '*Christliche*' or Christian virtue. Religion and tolerance were not so far removed from each other, as somebody like Ernst Bloch would say, they never are. But if you read *Kalyan*, you will not recognize the religion that most of us belong to. It talks all kinds of nonsense; it quotes ten *richas* from the *Yajurveda* or somewhere similar. On the left, the Sanskrit text is printed and on the right, its Hindi translation. And even my kind of Sanskrit is good enough to see that the translation does not match the original at all. And the claim made is that this is the first ever national anthem anywhere in the world! This is most extraordinary. In other words, they are trying to say that Hindus were a nation! And look, here is its national anthem! They call it *rashtrageet*. *Rashtra* is usually translated as 'nation' in most Indian languages. Originally, the term appears in the *Rigveda* and there the meaning of the word is extremely limited: a territory governed by a king. It does not have anything to do with the 'nation-state' as we understand it today. The funny part of it is that nobody is going to ask them a question; nobody is even willing to make fun of them.

I could go on multiplying such examples but I hope the point is clear. There has been a systematic attack on the culture of tolerance. But the battle was never joined in, or so it appears. It seems that the liberals and the radicals—that is to say, you and me—don't join in battles. And when we don't, they hit us hard.

Speech delivered on 10 November 2003 at the 'Theatre Matters' forum, Prithvi Theatre Festival, Mumbai 2003

Notes towards a Re-reading of the Natyashastra

It is a singular honour to have been invited to deliver the Pablo Neruda Memorial Lecture. I know that I do not quite deserve to be speaking from this pulpit and on such an occasion. Were this the only problem one could have somehow or the other got over it. Friends like you would have helped me get over the initial hesitation and diffidence. But it is not the only problem. What makes my audacity even worse is that the honour the Centre and its council have chosen to do to me has placed me in the company of truly distinguished people who have spoken in the series before me. When I think of all this I feel like Arjuna as he stood on the battleground of Kurukshetra. *Seedanti mama gatrani, mukhancha parishushyati,* said he (my faculties have given way, my mouth has dried up) and went on to describe how his whole body shook, how he could barely control his excited nervousness. My state is no different.

My predecessors at this lectern have been, to use a typical Indian metaphor, *diggajas,* the protective elephant gods who defend the ten directions. As you know, the metaphor is now used in almost all Indian languages for the masters in a field. And indeed, each of them who have spoken before me have been people of much greater reputation than I can ever achieve, or ever dream of. These people know the direction of their thought. They know their world clearly and vividly. I do not know any direction. I am a typical *dishaviheen* (directionless) person.

Why, then, did I agree to speak, you must wonder. Well it is fairly simple. The people who asked me to do so are my personal friends. My respect for them makes it almost impossible to say no. It is a *dharmasankata* of a kind, a predicament which does not quite offer any escape. The temptation to associate with the memory of Pablo Neruda is irrestible. Perhaps it is an opportunity to repay a debt to an all-time great poet. So I thought I might well share with you 'the splendour of my confusion', to borrow Neruda's words. He concludes his poem 'Too Many Names' thus:

> I have a mind to confuse things,
> Unite them, make them new-born,
> Mix them up, undress them—

Well, I intend to do that to the *Natyashastra*!

Let me begin by stating what my project does not attempt to do. This is not a textual critique of the *Natyashastra*. This also means that I am not taking a typical Indological view of that text although, in a way, my view is Indological: a socio-political view of Indology is inherent in my perspective of that work. My concern can be summed up in one question or a set of cognate questions. Is it possible to take a fresh look at the *Natyashastra*? How does a modern playwright look or how should he look at that text? In other words, I hope to present, in its barest outline of course, a reading of the text that I have myself attempted over a period of time. It is hardly necessary to add that my discussion is limited to the chapters relating to drama. I have no intention of discussing those sections dealing with the other performing arts and there are two good reasons for so limiting my scope. The primary reason is that I am, basically, a theatre activist. A playwright and a small-time actor. This limits my interest. Secondly, my little reading of the text tells me that it is not only possible to look at that work as a compendium of sorts but also desirable to do so. In the case of a compendium, a partial view can at times be rather useful. It can make some insights available which might, in fact, throw considerable light on several aspects of the work which would be rather useful for an overall understanding of the text.

Having stated my initial qualifiers and caveats, let me now turn to the text. The *Natyashastra* was probably redacted some time between the first century BC to the first century AD. There is a story in its dating. Dr Manmohan Ghosh, an eminent Indologist, put together the first authentic edition of the work. In the first edition, Dr Ghosh placed the work in the period just mentioned. In the second edition, he dated the work differently, to circa fifth century BC. This means that the book was now half a millennium older. It is not entirely possible to explain the temporal jump in Dr Ghosh's dating. It is not as though Dr Ghosh did not offer any arguments in favour it. He did. But the evidence that he marshalled did not quite clinch the argument. In short, he was less than convincing. His arguments and their limitations need not detain us here. He published the second edition during the high tide of nationalism, a period when a certain Orientalism dominated the view of Indian history. That Orientalist approach, at least in its Indian adherents, seemed to take every ancient Indian work as far back in time as possible. It is possible that Dr Ghosh's new dating was a typical example of the complete internalization of that approach.

There is, however, another significance of the new dating. If we place the text in the fifth century BC, it becomes a pre-Greek text. The Ionian Greeks were nowhere near India at that time. Any suggestions of Greek influences on the *Natyashastra* thought on drama, and there were many, could then be dismissed as anachronisms. The *Natyashastra* uses the word *yavanika* for curtain. At one stage it was thought that the word could be traced to 'Ionian' (Greek). Now the chances are that such an etymological exercise was no more than an attractive theorization based on mere phonetic similarity between the words. It is possible that the two words are not related and that *yavanika* can be traced to some other root. But if the *Natyashastra* is dated well before the arrival of the Greeks in India, the problem is dissolved, as it were.

This argument about dating is, however, vital to where one places the Greeks historically. We see two connected approaches here. In India, especially in the twentieth century, there was an increasing tendency to view the Greeks as 'Europeans'. The nationalist logic demanded that a certain distance between India and Greece be established. It is possible to view Dr Ghosh's new dating of the *Natyashastra* in these terms. It is also a part of a larger phenomenon. What happened in India (as regards the Greeks) was a mirror image of what happened in Europe. There was an increasing tendency in Europe to make Greece as purely

European as possible. A typical example is Heidegger's view that the expression 'Western European philosophy' was tautological and that this European philosophy is 'inseparable from its historical constitution in the Greek intellectual and cultural world'. This meant that in this view there was a severance of ancient Greece from Asia. There was not even the consideration of the fact that if the Greeks had had no links with Asia there would not have been a play on the Persians, easily the most ancient play on the political and rather less than friendly interaction between Greece and a part of Asia. (It might be mentioned here in passing that Edward Said refers to this play in *Orientalism* contributing unwittingly to the process of 'Europeanization' of Greece.)

In one sense what happened was not entirely unnatural. From the time of Enlightenment, Europe has discovered the world and itself. In colonial societies there was, likewise, a great voyage of self-discovery. What I have cited above regarding the new dating of the *Natyashastra* and the appropriation of Greece by Europe were part of the projects of self-definition that we were witness to in both Europe and India. That made them and us the 'other' of each other. We should understand Dr Ghosh's new dating in these terms, as a part of what I have described as 'dialectics of defeat' elsewhere. This means that there is a politico-historical element in our (for that matter their) revisiting of the old texts. I submit that this is what happened in the process of the dating of the *Natyashastra*. Now, of course, we have a general consensus that the date of the *Natyashastra* is between the first century BC and the first century AD while some parts of the compendium attributed to Bharata Muni (traditionally identified as the author of the *Natyashastra*; we do not know much about him or whether he was the author or a compiler of the *Natyashastra*) may have been composed earlier. This would demonstrate the need to historicize all such arguments. This is all the more necessary if we wish to understand reasonably clearly the thrust of a given text and what it wishes to argue. No text stands alone. It has important predecessors.

Let me now turn to one such predecessor. It is well known that the central notion in the *Natyashastra* is that of the rasa. The

Natyashastra also mentions that there are eight rasas. (Abhinavagupta in his ninth-century commentary on the *Natyashastra, Abhinavabharati,* added the ninth rasa, the *shanta* rasa). Let us now turn to the *Chhandogya Upanishad* which belongs to the *Sama Veda.* This Veda has few independent verses (*richas*). It is an Upanishad of the Chhandoga (the singer of the *Sama*). The word is derived thus: *chhando sama gayati iti chhandogah.* As you can see, the text is addressed to a performer, explaining to him what *chhanda* he sings and why. It talks of rasas. The syllable of *aum* is the *udgeetha.* Every recital of the Vedic chants has to begin with that syllable. Interestingly, this performative *udgeetha* has been described thus: *saesha rasanam rasatamah paramah parardhyoshtamo udgeethah.* (That is the quintessence of the essences, the Supreme, the highest, the eighth, namely the *udgeetha*).

Please note the use of the term rasa. It is called the essence of essences. The *Natyashastra* uses the term rasa as the quintessence of the aesthetic experience. The terms *chhanda* and rasa are thus linked. The *udgeetha* is called the eighth. Did the count of rasas in the *Natyashastra* come to be eight because the *udgeetha* was the eighth? It is a plausible hypothesis. (I have used here Dr H. R. Bhagvat's version of this Upanishad published in 1914, which used the adjective *manorathi* for the *udgeetha.*) This word is to be found in a number of Indian languages. It may not be necessary to translate it here. Suffice it to say that the word would firmly relate the chanting to imagination. (*Manorathi* literally means somebody whose mind races ahead like a chariot—in other words, a sharply imaginative person.) In short, creativity is under discussion here.

In the second section, the Upanishad talks about the interaction between the gods (*devas*) and the demons (*asuras*). It goes on to say that the *devas* worshipped the *udgeetha.* But then the *asuras* interfered in the process of worship, so to speak, with their sinful touch. The result was that it became possible to think of both the thinkable and the unthinkable, *sankalpaniya* and *asankalpaniya.* The chapter goes on to discuss polarities like fragrance and odour. The *Chhandogya* is thus talking of mutually constituting opposites. It also defines the *devas* and the *asuras. Deva* stands for the *indriya vritti* (physical tendencies) enlightened by the sciences. The *asur-*

as, on the other hand, represent the *indriya vrittis* devoted to material pleasure. If you think hard enough you will realize that no art is possible without the latter kind of the *indriya vrittis.* This means that it is through the interaction of the *devas* and the *asuras* and later, between the *savarnas* and the shudras, that the business of chanting, i.e. singing, and indeed the business of performing arts, has been possible. In fact, in one place in the *Natyashastra,* it has been stated in no uncertain terms that theatre is the business of the shudras. So, going by the dictates of the *Natyashastra,* I am a shudra. Small wonder that it is so. All beautiful and useful things were practised by the shudras. Take medicine, for example. It was the *ambasthas* who practised medicine and they were shudras. When I thought about this I felt that this is a relationship of conflict or contradiction, if you will, and that the *Natyashastra* was trying to make that point. It is contradiction and therefore *sangharsha* which makes art possible. Then, one turned to other texts like the *Chhandogya* which said that the nose did not know odour till it discovered it through contact with the *asuras.* 'Then they meditated on the *udgeetha* as the breath in the nose. The demons affected that with evil. Therefore, with it one smells both the sweet-smelling and the foul-smelling, for it is afflicted with evil'. The *devas* had known only the fragrance. They had the monopoly of it, as it were. It is only evil which made the knowledge of odour possible, the *papa* (evil) that is. If we thought this argument out we would discover that there would be no fragrance without odour. It is dialectic of a kind. And the role of the shudras establishes it. There would not have been any drama or any art for that matter if this interaction had not been there. The *Natyashastra* makes theatre the business of the shudras. Here, we are face to face with one long tradition of contradiction and creativity.

Sometimes I feel that this effect of evil has probably something to do with performance as well. The day the *papa* touches an actor or a singer he comes up with a sterling performance. The *Chhandogya* talks about it. So does the *Natyashastra.*

I think Bernard Shaw has spoken of tedium somewhere. A good drama will and should produce tedium. How does one distinguish between tedium and boredom? One might give a

Chhandogya kind of answer to that question. Tedium is generated by the touch of the *papa*. It pins you down; it does not let you go. Boredom lets you turn away from it. Tedium generates *krodha*, the thinking man's anger. The *asura* touch, as it were. This notion of the polluting (*papamana*) contact with the *asura*, or by extension, the shudra, is fascinating. The *Chhandogya* suggests it. The *Natyashastra* confirms it by stating that a theatre person is a shudra.

Anyway, to return to the business of tedium, in our context it is related to *krodha* or uneasiness. When you read Phule's play written in 1855, you would be very uneasy or extremely angry depending upon your understanding of nineteenth-century Hinduism. In other words, tedium makes you think. The play must entertain and at the same time, make you think. Thinking is the beginning of understanding. *Yada vai manute, atha vijarrati*, the *Chhandogya* again. When one thinks, then one understands. I suggest that the *Natyashastra* position would not be different.

It may be useful to look once again at the story from the *Natyashastra* about how the idea of the auditorium originated. After the violence subsided between the clashing members of the audience, Brahma suggested that there should be an auditorium to perform in, presumably with a view to limit any disturbance prompted by the performance within a well-defined space. It is clear from the story that the narrative of the play was in contradiction with the *asura* world-view. When each *asura*, at least a great number of them, began thinking about it, they understood it. In the *Natyashastra* view, drama i.e. creativity and conflict, were and are intricately linked. It seems to me that this perspective provided by the *Natyashastra* has been generally ignored by most contemporary readings of that text. Hence, the need of a re-reading.

Equally important is the other perspective that the *Natyashastra* and the Indian tradition provide on the nature of drama according to which, drama or theatre is not real but *kritaka*, i.e. false or unreal. We can also say that the reality in theatre is the reality of the *chitraturaga nyaya. Chitra* is a picture. *Turaga* is a horse. Is the horse in the picture real? Well, 'yes and no' would be the answer. It is real in the sense that we can recognize the horse in the picture as a horse. It is unreal in the sense that we cannot ride it. In other words, the material reality of the horse makes the artistic reality of the horse in ancient Indian *Kalaavichara* (thinking on the arts)—from the *Chitrasutra* (a treatise on painting) to the *Natyashastra.* This is no small wonder for the society which had a special place for *anityata* (non-performance, the term for dialectic in Buddhist philosophy). I draw your attention to this tradition for two reasons. One, I want to emphasize how alive the text of the *Natyashastra* and other texts of criticism once were before becoming fossilized. Two, the *Natyashastra* approach rejects naturalism. Indeed, the entire ancient tradition of literary and art criticism does so.

One should perhaps add that this is also true of medieval India. Abhinavagupta wrote his commentary one thousand years after the *Natyashastra.* He also celebrated the anti-naturalistic tradition. There is some point in referring to medieval India in this regard. His writing is fairly close to the rise of Indian vernaculars, which it influenced. If Sanskrit was the language of the *devas,* the vernaculars were the languages of the *asuras*! No wonder he made an immediate impact on them. The contribution of this scholar of the Kashmir Shaiva School was, in the main, the propounding of the ninth, *shanta* rasa. His theory found a ready response among the vernacular writers of who a good example would be Dnyaneshwar, the thirteenth-century Bhakti poet writing in Marathi, celebrating the *shanta.* One contrasts this to the tenth rasa proposed by a brahmanical Sanskrit scholar, Madhusudan Saraswati, a figure referred to in an earlier essay. This scholar was the contemporary of Tulsidas yet his discussion of the Bhakti rasa does not even refer to Tulsidas, let alone the Bhakti tradition of medieval India. It is difficult to think of another example of literary or aesthetic theorization which is so unmindful of the contemporary literary praxis.

There is another formulation of Abhinavagupta in his commentary on the *Natyashastra.* It comes fairly close to what most modern Indians have learnt from Brecht. I mean the Brechtian theory of the actor's distancing from his role. What does an actor do when he plays Macbeth? He does not become Macbeth. He demonstrates Macbeth. In other words, he distances himself from Macbeth. Now consider what Abhinavagupta said in his commentary. He says: *paatram tarhi kim? Aswadatopayah. Paatra* has two meanings in Sanskrit and, therefore, in several Indian languages. One is character in a play and the other, a vessel. So Abhinavagupta warned the actor that he was merely an instrument of enjoyment. He cannot and should not identify with the character in a way that he becomes that character. A vessel or a glass (*paatram*) carrying the wine does not become drunk. That *paatra* is the ideal of the actor. In his commentary on the eleventh chapter of the *Bhagawat Purana*, Eknath describes acting thus: *nata angi rajvilasu tari to rajaullasu nata na manee.* (An actor is luxuriously dressed as a king. Yet he does not make the mistake of believing that he is the king himself.)

The Bhakti movement had taken a view of acting that was very similar to Abhinavagupta's. It is obvious that Eknath was a part of the people's movement of the Bhakti and, as such, must have observed the contemporary performing practice of his people. The same must be true of Abhinavagupta and his commentary on the *Natyashastra.*

It is amazing but true that we have forgotten the near-revolutionary thinking of *Natyashastra*, Abhinavagupta and the medieval traditions of the Indian vernaculars. It would seem that imperialism taught us to look at ancient thought as if it were pure, sacred and the like. It also pushed the thinking in the vernaculars of the medieval period under the rug. These texts were revived later, more as a form of our Orientalism. But no attempt was made to relate these texts to the linguistic and artistic experience of the people. The early approaches to the *Natyashastra* were not very different from Madhusudan Saraswati's approach to Bhakti. He knew Narada's *Bhakti Sutras* but had no use for Tulsidas or his Bhakti. This is a sure way of fossilizing ideas and texts. It is important to fight such fossilized and therefore 'pure' versions of theatre being advocated presently by many in our country. It can only lead to revivalism.

Why does this approach get perpetuated? It does, I think, because of the disjunction between the vernacular, Sanskrit and Western traditions. Those who know the Sanskrit tradition do not know the Western tradition. Those who know the Western tradition do not know the Sanskrit tradition. And both of them do not know the vernacular tradition of the medieval age. We have to fight this emphasis on the pure and the sacred. We must revive the 'contact with the evil'.

We have, in our country, failed to see the cultural crisis that faces us squarely. The problem is not one of cultural nationalism. It is rather to fight an Orientalist cultural memory. All texts cry out for re-reading and the *Natyashastra* certainly does so.

Such a reading has to begin with Abhinavagupta. I have already mentioned that Abhinavagupta was a Shaivaite. He has a commentary on Shaiva *darshana.* This detail (rather slight at first view) is, in fact, quite central to his philosophical and metaphysical position. Among other things, Kashmir Shaivism is stoutly against *varna* and caste. His commentary on the *Natyashastra* cannot be fully understood without keeping this aspect of Shaivism in view. No less important is the Sankhya school of philosophy which is quite noticeable in the *Natyashastra.* In that school there are two quite central concepts of *bhojya* (worthy of consumption) and the *bhokta* (consumer). It is the duality which is at the centre of the appreciation (consumption) of art. This would suggest that this formulation places the material, i.e. the consumable, world at the centre of the art enterprise. This view moves away from the Vedanta. It moves away from its metaphysics of art experience. It disqualifies *swarga* (this term is usually translated as paradise but it involves unnecessary confusion of categories; it is better to translate it as the land of the gods) from the realm of theatre! It argues that theatre can happen only where there is *duhkha* (sorrow or suffering). *Swarga* as the land of the gods cannot possible know *duhkha.* If one were to extend the *Natyashastra* logic, one could suggest a possible explanation of the *Natyashastra* aphorism. Not knowing *duhkha* is not knowing the material world, for it is only in the material world or the world of the mortals or the world here and now that anyone can know *duhkha.* Abhinavagupta extends the logic a step forward. He recommends that India is the land of theatre because it is the land of *duhkha.* One can see that the *Natyashastra* and Abhinavagupta positions in certain terms are very materialistic. It presents an antithesis of the idealistic view of the performing arts generally and of theatre particularly.

But then there is also an idealistic part of the *Natyashastra.* We can thus see two schools of thought in the *Natyashastra.* The first of the two, the materalist one, is connected with violence. It is also related with the shudras and the *asuras.* The other school is idealist. It is the idealism of the other school which sustains the rasa theory.

This means that there are, in fact, two books within one treatise called the *Natyashastra.* One follows the materialistic logic, of course, in a limited sense. We can also talk of a certain social consciousness that is very apparent in one book. The other book is an idealistic piece of writing. It talks of the rasa. Let me take you back once again to the *Chhandogya.* It says that *udgeetha* or *aum* should be worshipped. And then it goes on to analyse the world in terms of the rasa (essence) of everything. The essence of being is earth. The essence of earth is water. The essence of a person is speech. The essence of speech is the *rik* (hymn). The essence of the hymn is the *saman* (chant). The essence of the chant is the *udgeetha.* The *Chhandogya* thus speaks of the eight rasas. S. Radhakrishnan translates rasa as 'essence' or 'flavour'. The Marathi translation I have used explains rasa as *sara* (essence) or *adhara* (support or that which sustains). To the best of my knowledge, the use of the concept of rasa in the *Chhandogya* should be the earliest reference to rasa in Sanskrit. It is significant that the reference occurs in the context of chanting or singing, i.e. in the context of a performing art. I do not know for certain if the rasa of the *Natyashastra* is related to the rasa of the *Chhandogya.* However, it seems to me likely that the two concepts are related. It is interesting that the 1914 (Marathi) translation uses the notion of adharma, which is also the basis of dharma: *dharayati asau sa dharmah* (what sustains is dharma). It is quite customary to use the term dharma to indicate duty or code, whether religious or secular. This makes it very likely that we have to trace the word rasa from the Upanishads through the *Natyashastra*. It is easy to see that even the discussion of rasa in the *Natyashastra* is twofold. It is a combination of the idealistic approach and the sheer experiential world of arts. In the case of the latter, the rasa would be aesthetic experience. In case of the former, it would be a formal aesthetic doctrine, clearly related to the aesthetics, the Greek word, that makes aesthetics at least etymologically a subjective concept.

I do not intend going into the discussion of the doctrine of rasa like *bhavas* and *vyabhichari bhavas* and so on. All those details are easily available in several books. My point is that the *rasa siddhanta* (the doctrine of rasa) is the idealistic part of the *Natyashastra*. I do not see how we can really take it as valid today. The theatre of modernity, for example, would be scarcely understood or appreciated in terms of rasa. You cannot really look at any modern play or a poem in any useful way in those terms. I had once seen a discussion of a long poem by Wordsworth in the language of ancient Indian literary thought. It was an amusing if not a particularly productive exercise. If this is true of a romantic poem you can imagine how absurd an exercise of looking at a modern play or a poem in terms of *rasa siddhanta* would be. In that sense, one of the most famous critics of modern India, the late D. K. Bedekar was right when he argued that the *rasa siddhanta* had to be seen as a beautiful museum piece.

However, there is the other aspect of the *Natyashastra*. It is also a performer's handbook. It is also a spectator's handbook. And this is the materialist aspect of that work. Once the book is understood in terms of performance and its enjoyment, we inevitably turn to its social and material character. We have already referred to violence and the like. Here, the Sankhya concepts like *bhojya* and *bhokta* become central. All this relates to *indriya vritti* and *asuras*.

To use a modern term, the *Natyashastra* lays down a reception-aesthetics. It makes the actor conscious of the fact that he is out here to deliver something which is to be consumed here and now by the spectator. It reminds me a bit of Stanislavsky's much celebrated treatise *An Actor Prepares.* The *Natyashastra* is a book of the *gestus,* or gesture in drama, a term made popular by Brecht and which he rated even higher than the spoken word. In other words, the book is all about the business on stage, or about theatrical praxis. As such the *Natyashastra* is a functional and practical book. Its materiality cannot, however, be understood without reference to the unreal reality that commentators like Abhinavagupta, Bhattanayaka and Sankuka were talking about.

But before we proceed further, let me reiterate that it is necessary to think of the *Natyashastra* as essentially two books. At any rate the commentators have questioned the *rasa siddhanta* mainly in terms of the experience of the here and now. Bhattanayaka raised an important question. If the rasa is generated through experience the question is, whose experience? Is it the experience of the spectator who uses his logical faculties or is it the experience of the author or is it the experience of the actor? Or is it the function of all three? The even more important question is the one of cognisance. For him it was an epistemological project, or so it would appear. In his view, when a spectator sees a play, his experience is both enjoyment and, to use a simple Indian word, *jnanavyavahara* or an epistemological project. One does not even know if the Indian tradition at all talks of *saundaryashastra* or aesthetics. It probably does not. We have *sahityashastra* or the science of painting and so on. Acharya Hazariprasad Dwivedi prefers the word *lalitya* and I think that there is a point in it. (His famous book on Kalidasa is called *Kalidasa ki Lalityayojana.*)

This is so because of the centrality of the word in theatre. It is so central that in the *Natyashastra* we do not find any discussion of silences anywhere. There is some discussion of certain characters not listening in to certain other characters. Some gestures called the *patakas* are to let the spectator know of the intended partial communication. But of meaningful silences there is no discussion at all. In our times, theatre depends more and more on silences. Indeed, the word is becoming increasingly a difficult, if not an impossible, commodity to handle. The best example of the modern inadequacy of the word is the dramatic world of Beckett. His plays became increasingly smaller. Pinter said once that he would probably write only one-act plays now. Think now of what Eliot says in *Four Quartets*:

> Words strain,
> Crack and sometimes break, under the burden,
> Under the tension, slip, slide, perish,
> Decay with imprecision, will not stay in place,
> Will not stay still.
>
> ('Burnt Norton', *Four Quartets*)

In other words, the word is fast becoming unusable, unemployable. The word is getting broken into pieces, as it were. This predicament of the word is connected with industrial societies and the barrenness they generate everywhere. In such a situation rasa simply cannot be generated. It is an anachronism. If it is and can in fact be generated it will be the rasa of the *Chhandogya*. It will require a movement to *paramatman* or 'the cosmic being'. It will not be the rasa of the *Natyashastra*.

So there you are. There are two books. There are two *rasa siddhantas*. It is a bit like breaking up. Think of the famous line from *King Lear*: 'it splits, it splits, it splits'. Moretti, the famous Italian critic, has read *Lear* as a play of the disintegration of sovereignty. And indeed, we live in times of disintegration. In these hard times it is increasingly hazardous, if not impossible, to make sense of words, of complete, holistic philosophies or theories.

This raises then the crucial question: should we or have we got to distinguish between the modern and the pre-modern theories? In other words, what does one do with the forever-splitting world of experience and of language? Related to this is the question as to what we make of the Sanskrit tradition. Paradoxically, a number of meaningful comments in Abhinavagupta commentary are precisely those which turn the metaphysics of well-known, almost axiomatic observations on their heads. The *Gita* speaks of death and rebirth as if they were the *atman* giving up old clothes for new. Abhinavagupta uses this verse in an almost subversive way to argue that an actor does precisely that when he moves from one role into another. It re-emphasizes the distancing too, a very modern emphasis indeed. It is the 'social and material' *Natyashastra* that distances itself from Vedantic metaphysics. It is this distancing which gives it the perspective on the actor's distancing from the role. This may be the reason why there has been no discussion about the *Natyashastra* and the Abhinavagupta position on distancing, although nothing could have been more explicit. The only explanation for this then is that our pandits do not like the subversion of the Vedantic metaphysics that is inevitably involved in that view.

There is also a further reason for this lapse. During colonial times it was perhaps a necessity to assert that our civilization had formulations on everything, as fine as they get. In our polemical zeal, we tended to ignore the anti-Vedantic formulations and postures. Our understanding of the *Natyashastra* and Abhinavagupta is of that kind. The net result was that the two *Natyashastras* that we talked about became one.

We then argued with colonizing Europe if you will. Look, if you have your Aristotle, we have our Bharata and Abhinavagupta. The crucial difference, however, was that Aristotle has been a living reality for them. We were not even certain what the *Natyashastra* and Abhinavagupta had to argue. Consequently, the more *anityatavadi* aspects of the *Natyashastra* and Abhinavagupta were forgotten or were ignored. I think that the performing arts experience of the Indian people, especially in theatre, is an experience of our vernaculars and most of them originated in the medieval period. If there had been continuous interaction between the experiential and the creative world of the Indian languages and texts like the *Natyashastra* it would have been a different story. But that was not to be.

The point however is to retrieve the social and the material in our tradition. We can then see the plural tradition that is inherent in the ancient texts. I have offered these notes very tentatively. I am not certain how useful or meaningful they are. I can only request you to forget this evening if all that I have said does not amount to much of coherence or value.

The Fifth Pablo Neruda Lecture delivered at the Developing Countries Research Centre, University of Delhi, 2003

Europe and Our Theatre

1

A Croatian play being presented in Marathi in this city of the Peshwas that has had a special relationship with modernity is an event of historical significance. It has opened a new chapter in the history of modern Marathi and, therefore, Indian theatre. I refer to modernity advisedly. We do not usually talk of our modern theatre when we speak of the so-called Indian theatre. It is strange but true that the discourse of 'Indian Theatre' in our country has had a rather tenuous relationship with modernity. Consider the presidential addresses of the much-celebrated *sahitya sammelans* (annual literary congregations, of doubtful value according to many). Rarely do they mention any significant play or playwright when they make their assessments of the contributions to Marathi literature. Not many of these worthies consider the theatre of modernity as legitimate literature or so it would appear. The so-called *akshar sahitya* (literature that will last) does not seem to include the theatre of modernity.

Against this background, the welcome accorded to a play from the Balkans deserves special appreciation. There is an interesting dialogue in one of the Wodehouse novels. Bertie Wooster asks Jeeves, as the famous butler brings the morning paper to his master, if there is anything interesting or noteworthy in the papers. Jeeves replies, 'Nothing in particular, the Balkans are quiet'. It makes for ironic reading in our times as the Balkans have not been quiet, for the last God knows how many decades. In India, the cultural presence of the states which constituted what was once known as Yugoslavia has been even more of a rarity. The last major cultural news from this region to have reached us was when an author from Bosnia, Croatia's neighbour and who uses the same language for literary expression as Croatia, got the Nobel Prize in 1961. Ivo Andric was a Bosnian by birth, lived in Belgrade and, presumably wrote in Serbo-Croat. The matter was reported in the press, that's all. I read about him much later in a book on the cultural history of the region. This author has been variously described. One description that has stuck in my mind is that of his 'perfectionist aesthetics'. To celebrate aestheticism in the era of socialist realism, albeit in its declining years, was extraordinary. Apart from that, we have had hardly any news of literary happenings along the Adriatic coast. This play and its reading in Pune are therefore news of great import.

It might be useful to use this occasion to take a look at our interaction with European theatre.

2

Our first brush with 'modern' theatre was in 1795 when a Russian director produced a play (in English) in Calcutta. The cast was entirely European. I do not recall what play it was. But that is not material to our account. The point is that the 1795 performance could be identified as our first exposure to European theatre language and, thereby, to modernity. It is important to see that this performance belongs to what could be described as the age of reformation, in a manner of speaking, in our country—Raja Rammohun Roy and his times. This view must appear to many as an exercise in viewing history as a grand narrative. The postmodernists would reject it out of hand whereas to many others this must seem no more than an unjustified effort at seeing connections which are at best tenuous and at worst, wild. Be that as it may, European theatre has not left us alone since. Let us use this occasion of the play from the Balkans visiting us to take an overall view, a *vihangamavalokan* (bird's-eye view) of sorts, of the interaction between Europe and the emerging modern theatre in the languages of India. Interestingly, this interaction has moved from West to East, from the Atlantic and, shall we say in the context of the Croatian play, to the Adriatic. In ancient times, there was some exchange between India and the Ionian Greeks. As is well known, the Sanskrit word for the foreigner, *yavana*, is clearly a derivation of Ionian. With the age of colonialism and, I must say also of modernity, the focus shifted to the West. This was the time when we discovered Shakespeare. There is one major difference between our discovery of the Bard and Jan Kott's discovery of him. The Polish critic discovered in him a contemporary. We discovered in him an icon. In a sense the colonies helped the British to transform him thus, both for the metropolis and the colonies themselves, a fascinating example of what Sartre has called the 'relentless reciprocity (which) binds the colonizer and the colonized'. The Shakespeare Day that has come to be celebrated in Britain since 1916 is a phenomenon inextricably connected with its idea of Empire. It is extraordinary how the idea of imperial monarchy was linked to the celebration of Shakespeare. A standard and perhaps mandatory way of celebrating the day was to perform a scene or two from his plays followed by 'God Save the King'! There is a rather educative account of this in that slightly irreverent piece of writing called 'The Political Shakespeare'. But then, let it not detain us for too long. Suffice it to say that our relationship with him has not been natural. Hindu society can and does turn everybody and anybody into a godhead and that is what happened to Shakespeare. You may or may not have read him or seen him on stage but you adore him anyway.

One consequence of this was that our relationship with English theatre was not natural. We had to look up at it, our necks raised! Unlike Kott we did not, indeed could not, look at Shakespeare as our contemporary. In fact, in our poor imitation of the so-called Shakespearean prose, we simply transformed our prose styles and, as many have argued, made them worse. A typically sardonic description of that style was 'Anglo-Brahmanical'. We need not go into the polemical zeal of that apostrophe. The basic point was right; for the new style moved away from the spoken word in complete disregard of Shakespeare's use of the everyday language of his time and, at times, rough usage. Most of our admirers of Shakespeare would be unhappy that in the introduction to his anthology of Shakespearean nuggets Ted Hughes should have celebrated his 'virtuoso development of the poetic instincts of English dialect'. And no wonder. It is not easy to see the colonizer's language as a dialect! In fact, a typical aspect of the Shakespearean impact on the colonial scene was that the poetic instincts were forgotten. The ornate quality of that dramatic language comes from that historical relationship with colonialism. One should also mention here the fact that Shakespeare's histories completely escaped our attention, which is a pity. There is a remarkable lack of understanding of what history is and how it should be presented. Realistic speech was given the go-by and its place was taken by ornate speech. It has taken quite long for Marathi dramatic speech, for example, to get over the reconstructed vernacular Shakespeare. I suppose, because we were required to take a look at the marvel of our colonial masters, we had to view it from below. The net result was that we were denied a realistic view of the Bard. I get the feeling always that there are two Shakespeares, maybe three. The first is, of course, *the* Shakespeare who wrote the plays. The second is the one created by the Empire through the Shakespeare Days. The third is the received Shakespeare. We could not have got the right view of him as he was (and still is) on a pedestal. Shaw's attacks on him did not make sense to anyone here. We grew used to looking at European theatre as if it existed at a distant height. We had to stretch our necks! And you will agree that to keep our necks stretched for over two centuries is bound to be more than painful.

It is not as though there were no playwrights who could be viewed at one's own level. Shaw was one of them. But the problem was that when it came to European theatre we could not negotiate authors who had little or no use for the Empire. I cannot immediately think of anyone other than Utpal Dutt and Satyadev Dubey who have done Shaw. Both have been ideological animals, of course, but at the opposite ends of the spectrum, one should hasten to add. Much as we might celebrate modernity, we cannot ignore its dialectic. The modern play worked a modernity of sorts but it also perpetuated a certain iconic system in a typical colonial setting. It prevented us from looking at the Bard as a playwright. It is not as though there were no sceptics here too. A review of a translation, if my memory does not fail me, of *Cymbeline* (translated as *Tara*) by the celebrated essayist Chiplunkar in the nineteenth century made a lot of fun of our approach to Shakespeare's writing. Indeed, it would be a very rewarding exercise to do a comparative study of the Marathi and Bangla translations of Shakespeare in the late nineteenth and early twentieth century. The icon also prevented us from looking at continental writing. I wonder if there are any translations of Racine or even of a contemporary like Dürrenmatt. There is some point in mentioning this in Pune because this city has had a tradition of French and German studies of close to a century. How and why, then, the west European tradition should have got left out is a mystery. Anyway, the point is that this early fascination for the Anglo-Saxon has strangely persisted. This has resulted in our early modernist theatre being a Theatre of Imitation; at times imitation of a kind which did no justice either to the English or to us. There, too, we were stuck with at best the Victorian times and values. Even Harold Pinter and John Osborne were left out, presumably because we did not look back in anger at our habit of looking at the Victorian world through the brahmanical prism. All this was bound to stay with us for a while. It still does and will probably stay far longer than one would like. But then, there are no instant literary revolutions. Anyway, there is a bright side to the historical movement that we are talking about.

We have moved away, to an extent, from the stifling language that once passed as the new or standard language and have suddenly woken up to the reality of theatre-language. Our theatre began with and because of the British. It has, however, reached new heights when at least some of us started to live down that heritage. Presumably, as a part of that process, we discovered the Americans. Names like Arthur Miller, Tennessee Williams and even David Mammet became familiar. At least some members of the theatre community had at long last got over the historical obsession of the colonial period. There is a more realistic and less iconic approach to Shakespeare. Now there are performances of Shakespeare which speak a different language, a language of theatre rather than that of iconography. Suddenly a new view and new nuances are visible.

Good examples (not the only ones) would be the productions of *King Lear* and *Midsummer Night's Dream.*

The first phase of our theatre encounter with the West was thus dominated by contradictory relationships and perspectives. Europe provided us with a breath of fresh air. It looked as if the stagnant history had finally started moving. At the same time, imperialism distorted that relationship in a fundamental way. I have already described that distortion with the metaphor of viewing with our necks outstretched. It is not a normal view and it created a history of its own which had to be left behind as much as the stagnant history we had allegedly inherited.

3

The second phase of interaction with Europe begins well after India's freedom. This happens with our discovery of Brecht. It also marked our discovery of 'socialist Europe' to which, incidentally, Croatia—as a part of Yugoslavia—once belonged.

In many ways this interaction was, at least, partially liberating. The burden of the English heritage had already become much too heavy and its contribution to our creativity had reached its limits. We were already looking for new pastures. Brecht made his intervention at that time. A good decade after his death, he came alive in India's theatres. Marathi had its encounter with Brecht too. People like P. L. Deshpande and Khanolkar, themselves playwrights, came forward to adapt his plays for the Marathi stage and sensibility. The 'Mac the Knife' of *The Threepenny Opera* made quite an impact. P. L. Deshpande, easily the most subtle and sensitive translator/ adapter in Marathi, seems to have thoroughly enjoyed turning a Brechtian opera into a Deshpandian Tamasha, a great folk theatre form so typical of Maharashtra. This adaptation served yet another unintended purpose. Tamasha as a form had become a little jaded; it needed a new breath of life. But, before we proceed further, let me reiterate that the term 'folk' can be and indeed is a little misleading. That term assumes a divide between folk art and high art. Such a distinction would not be applicable to a number of Indian folk forms. A whole genre of Marathi poetry called *Shahiri kavita* has originated and prospered along with and as an integral part of Tamasha. I have elsewhere proposed, recently, that these forms may be more meaningfully called subaltern.

Without our knowing it, perhaps Brecht was undergoing a change in our midst. One must historicize the Brecht phenomenon in our country. It is not possible to draw a national picture in such a short space and time. Nevertheless, some observations can be made. It is a different India, a different Maharashtra, for that matter, that we encounter in the phenomenon of Brecht-reception. Because of the three economic development plans we see a lot of prosperity here. Incidentally, western India benefited most from this prosperity. Cities like Pune changed in a fundamental way with the beginning of the sixties. The dominant cultural class in the urban centres of Maharashtra was, at one time, the lower middle class with memories of the countryside, or 'memories of underdevelopment', if you will. Now that the lower middle class (made almost exclusively of upper-caste people at the time we are talking of) was on the decline, these upper-caste people had either lost those memories or had no use for them. They survived only as nostalgia, a nostalgia which P. L. Deshpande's writing quintessentially represents.

We received Brecht in that frame of mind. For us, Brecht also became a part of that nostalgia. Think of the use that Deshpande made of thirteenth-century writing like Dnyaneshwar's *Pasyadana* in his adaptation of *The Threepenny Opera.* The point that I am trying to make is that we made Brecht a definite part of our cultural heritage by almost transforming him into a Marathi playwright. Or, to put the same thing differently, the Marathi adaptations of Brecht have to be looked at as independent plays. They have little to do with his world-view and do not show any sign of 'the aesthetic of opposition' (*Aesthetik des wiederstandes*), to put the matter in terms of the title of a latter-day German novel. We made the systemic conflict ever present in his plays quite redundant. There was no post-modernism in those days. Otherwise, we could have well described these experiments as post-modern Brecht!

But there was more to the Brecht phenomenon than that. In a peculiar way he became the vehicle of the cultural nationalism of our people. It seemed that this well-to-do and alienated urban elite discovered its cultural forms and were quite excited that there was now an European sanction to the celebration of the 'subaltern' as it were. It was a voyage of self-discovery. We produced non-political and nostalgic Brecht. It was very enjoyable theatre, but scarcely Brechtian. It was cultural nationalism in the realm of the performative. (Let me add that I do not here use the category of cultural nationalism in the political meaning that is given to the term in India and, indeed, in a number of Third World states.)

We can, hopefully, see that our second encounter with Europe turned out to be yet another 'way of seeing', to borrow Berger's expression. In the first case we tried to look at Europe with elongated necks. In the second case, as we moved from the Anglo-Saxon world to *mitteleuropa*, we gave up looking at Europe and started looking at ourselves! 'The eyes became mirrors', as Dnyaneshwar put it in the thirteenth century. (A bad translation, I readily agree!) Let alone a way of seeing, it was no seeing at all.

4

We are now at the threshold of the third phase, or so it would seem. At any rate I see the significance of a Croatian play being presented in this city in those terms. The east of Europe has had a close relationship with India, which looks like a meeting of minds. Ancient Greece is a good example of it. May I cite a very minor but typical example from the philosophical traditions of the two countries? In the Hindu and Buddhist traditions the metaphor used for the human body is that of a chariot. The discussion is about how one decides what makes up the whole body (or anything for that matter). Is the whole equal to the parts? Or is it more than the parts? And so on. Is the chariot made of the parts? You find the same metaphor in Plato.

I am no philosopher. It is possible that I am reading too much into this. Professor Kapstein has dealt at some length with the Indian and the Greek chariot. The point simply is that the east of Europe is much closer to us than we or they imagine. Perhaps, the Aegean and the Adriatic Seas are closer to us than the Atlantic. It is possible that we can have a kind of level viewing at this part of Europe. No stretching of necks and no looking back at ourselves either!

There are several aspects of former Yugoslavian life which have a remarkable resemblance with our Indian experience. Both, India and Yugoslovia (even after the break-up of erstwhile Yugoslavia), are multinational states. There has been a problem of a dominant nationality in both their histories. The Croats and the Bosnians think of their history as that of struggle against Serbian dominance and, indeed, with considerable justification. This dominance is also noticeable in the recent history of the language. A Serbianization of language has been a constant theme. In a sense, the agreement on language arrived at Novi Sad in 1954 was a concession to Serbian cultural dominance. This was sought to be rectified in 1970 when an important meeting on 'The Serbo-Croatian Language' was held in Sarajevo.

I am no expert in the history of the area but what is fascinating about these developments is the concern for language and culture in that area. The Sarajevo conference also discussed new policies towards literary languages of the region.

Now this is fairly close to the experience in our own country. If in ancient times similar philosophical concerns made us speak of the same or similar concepts, today the comparable socio-political realities can start a new and rich dialogue between us. The point simply is that we may now relate to Europe in terms that are familiar to us. A cultural dialogue can begin. Commonness of problems can lead to a better understanding between people. Maybe this exchange of ideas will start the third encounter with Europe which will be rich, lasting and creative.

Keynote address delivered at the Croatia-Maharashtra Interaction Programme, 27–29 January 2004, Centre for Performing Arts, University of Pune

'Asia' as Western Dominance

There was once a very famous book entitled *Asia and Western Dominance* by historian-diplomat K. M. Panikkar. The book made quite a name when it first appeared more than fifty years ago. Now it is lost from memory. To be sure, it still does find mention in Ph.D. dissertations and books on modern Indian history. But it is no longer part of a living discourse either in Asia or elsewhere. In many ways, the language that Panikkar employed is almost forgotten. Nobody talks of Western dominance. There is an occasional reference to Asia but, unlike in the times of Panikkar's book, the term is not used in any political or cultural sense; it seems to be more of a geographic usage. When that book was written, everybody was certain of what Asia was and meant. Today, nobody is. Today, the term is used more to denote a land mass which is neither Europe nor Africa. Indeed, was there ever a meaningful reality called Asia?

It is interesting to note that most of the Indian languages, for example, the classical Indian languages like Sanskrit or Pali, do not or did not have a word for Asia. Modern Indian languages, some of which are more than a thousand years old themselves, do not either. What they do have is a coinage like *Ashiya* which is, really, a transliteration of 'Asia'. In other words, the Indian language world has no awareness of the Asia of pre-colonial times. I am not certain if the Chinese word for Asia, *Yazhou,* is also not merely a transliteration. A modern Chinese dictionary defines *Yazhou* merely as 'a word for Asia'. The classical Chinese tradition has hardly any awareness of Asia.

It is possible to argue that Europe created the notion or awareness of Asia. Asia for the Europeans was a world to discover and to dominate. Asia was, in that sense, a territory to be colonized. One can even say that, historically, Asia was, to use the Chinese word for Asia, *Ya*, which is 'inferior' or second in status. Europe invented Asia as an area to be occupied and exploited and, perhaps for that reason, to be celebrated. When the Suez Canal was opened in 1869, the Queen's representative spoke of connecting the two continents of Europe and Asia. Interestingly, he went on to add that the Canal would also link two periods of history. In his view, Asia belonged to an historical epoch while Europe, to the contemporary. The dominating colonialism was modern and contemporary and the dominated colonized was dated.

The world and word of Asia would have been discarded and forgotten if the phenomenon of Asia was limited to what the Queen's representative had said on that occasion. The colonial powers had made the interesting connection between the civilizational greatness of the lands they were going to rule or dominate and the historical need of that dominance for the colonized lands themselves. Lord Balfour had defended the British role in Egypt in these terms in 1908 or thereabouts (as I have mentioned in the first essay of this volume).

All this need not be regarded only as an exercise in cynicism as it no doubt was. There was an Orientalist view of the greatness of the 'other' necessarily involved in this exercise. The Orientalist scholarship of the eighteenth and the nineteenth century as also British and German romanticism had invented an Asia which the anti-colonial and anti-imperialist leadership, both political and cultural, had internalized. It was comforting and even flattering to see that European scholarship was interested in 'our' cultural achievements. The paradox of the situation was that it was the Europeans who were also introducing us to our own historical past. The German poet Goethe's apostrophe about Kalidasa's play *Shakuntalam* made us aware of the greatness of classical Sanskrit drama. A typical Asia-Europe relationship had begun. Europe defined Asia for us. We did not like it yet we lapped it up. For colonizing Europe, the notion of cultural and civilizational greatness was both a historical reality and an instrument of dominance. Asia as Western dominance was as much a reality as Asia *and* Western dominance.

The fact of the matter is that there is, in reality, no such entity as Asia. Even Orientalist scholarship estimated the several Asian civilizations differently; it was far more respectful of the Chinese civilization than it was of the Hindu-Bauddha or the Islamic, respectively, of the Indian sub-continent and the Arab-Persian world. Edward Said has argued that the thrust of the Orientalist scholarship was far more dismissive of the Middle-Eastern Islamic civilization than it was of the other civilizations. That may not be entirely true. The Hindu-Bauddha world was as much demonized as the Islamic. Perhaps the Chinese world partially escaped this demonization because of two reasons: it had escaped total colonization and there had been no rupture in its political tradition. The Confucian world remained a distant world which the European world was destined to only vaguely and respectfully understand as much as it could. James Legge, Jesuit missionary and translator of the Chinese classics, has made mention of the surprise many people express at his reverence for those works and then explained the basis of that emotion. No Indian classic has ever received such awe-inspiring respect. Even the Goethe apostrophe is qualified.

Europe thus invented not only Asia, but many Asias. We have to come to terms with these many partly real and partly unreal Asias. Asia is a myth. Certainly one Asia is. This is the reason why no pan-Asian movement ever succeeded. This is also the reason why Asian consciousness is on the decline if it has not already disappeared. A shared history of colonialism of barely a couple of centuries could not have made worlds of ideas of more than a couple of thousand years into a single world. And indeed it did not. The modern Asian mind remained torn between an imposed cultural and civilizational unity and actual divisions—at times, actual hostilities. India and Pakistan are a good example of this phenomenon. No two people, who have as much common between them as the people of these two states, have had a worse history of hostilities and distrust. Recent South Asian history is a standing refutation of the notion of Asia. There is a land mass called Asia. There are also billions of people called Asians. But these lands or these people have no common conception of Asia. Such notions of Asia as they have do not affect their daily life or their mutual relationships. They remain as distant from each other as possible.

Perhaps Europe needed the myth of Asia and its alleged definable quality in order to establish a distinct European identity. The first step in this exercise, of course, was to establish the myth of Asia. The second step was to sever the historical link between Greece and the Middle East. Modern Europe thus became a distinct Greco-Roman and Judeo-Christian civilization, which has now achieved a remarkable economic and political union. Asia was denied this chance of defining itself. The post-colonial dominance of Asia continues precisely because the conception of Asia as dominance persists. Whatever strength the Asian consciousness might have had during anti-colonial times, it has lost it completely during our globalization times. Europe (naturally inclusive of North America as it is an extension of Europe) is a 'unified reality' and Asia a divided land mass, a myth constantly challenged by its unreality.

It is also arguable that the myth of Asia in reality weakened the more palpable realities of civilizations. Europe needed this to happen. Europe does not wish to survive only as a strong economic and political union. It wishes to survive also as the dominating, the only civilization. We can think of the traditional world as made of many civilizations. Perhaps it was time to move away from the notions of land masses and retrieve the civilizations of these land masses. The Arab-Persian civilization or the Hindu-Bauddha-Indian-Islam civilization has to be consolidated. The world from the Mediterranean to China has lost its civilizational perspective. That fundamentalism of one variety or the other dominates this area is in itself an indication of the amnesia that this world suffers from. Curiously, fundamentalism is a Western invention. The West has carefully nurtured these notions and practices and has attacked them only when they have worked against its interests. The American tolerance of Saudi Arabian fundamentalism and its impatience with the Iranian variety are good examples. We have here a strange but interesting chain of developments. The myth of Asia also turned the history of Asia into a myth. All fundamentalism denies historical specificities and does not see the difference between, shall we say, the Muslims of Pakistan and those of Arabia. Or it cannot see the difference between the Christians of the Philippines and of, shall we say, Brazil. In the case of Europe, the totality of civilization brings the European people together, cementing them in a prosperous union. In the case of the so-called Asian lands, faith is the only decider of identities and, as such, divides the Asian people in an almost irreparable way. It would be foolhardy to deny the importance of faith. But it is and need not be the only decisive element of identity. I believe the Orientalist logic which described the Eastern (read Asian) people and traditions as essentially 'spiritual' (now thoroughly internalized) has been responsible for this loss of historical memory. These times of globalization make that amnesia worse.

The so-called Asian people thus live among the ruins of their civilizations. Their main battle is one of identity and where to locate it. The Islamic and the Hindu-Bauddha worlds are far away from victory in this battle if they have not already lost it. From Taliban to Vishwa Hindu Parishad, it is a long and painful story. But it would be an error not to see its historical and political roots. Equally, one should not forget the fact that the reconstruction of Asia under the aegis of colonizing Europeans was at least partially responsible for the present denouement. The earlier we give up the myth of Asia the better it would be.

As I have said before, China seems to have escaped this self-defeating identity crisis. It appears as if the Confucian civilization has been eminently successful in determining who the Chinese are and, perhaps more importantly, who they are not. There is no decline of faith in China (attacks on outfits like Fa Lun Gong notwithstanding) and yet faith is not a *sine qua non* of being Chinese. Confucian civilization is better able to face the challenge of globalization and Western civilization precisely because of its historicist view of itself. It would appear that they have matched the Hegelian and historicist view of itself of the Europeans. The Persians or the Arabs or the Indians and the Pakistanis have not done it yet. Indeed, vague notions of that sort do exist in all these areas, but they are so vague that they appear more often than not in a distorted manner. China and the Chinese people seem to be free of this.

It is very instructive to see the difference between the Chinese world and, shall we say, the South Asian world. During the heyday of the Empire, the myth of Asia had penetrated the world of ideas in South Asia. This was the reason why ideas like Pan-Asianism or Pan-Islamism held such sway in South Asia. China has never shared the perspective on Asia. There has been no 'Asia' as a decisive idea in the Chinese mind. There has only been China and the Chinese civilization and this has given them considerable strength.

Does it mean that the Chinese subscribe to the idea of 'clash of civilizations'? They do not. This is not the place to go into the thesis of 'the clash of civilizations'. But we should note that the theory at least partially serves the purpose of inducing such a clash —of course, to the immeasurable and inevitable advantage of the West. The current crisis involving Iraq is a case in point. If the concept of Asia served that purpose for imperialism and colonialism at one time, the concept of 'the clash of civilizations' serves the same purpose. It would appear that the Chinese leadership has grasped this fundamental truth.

We may be at the end of the period of Asia, Asia as Western dominance that is. Such 'Asian' states and people as see this clearly stand a chance of surviving the current Western drive of new initiatives at domination. If China is not alone in its undertaking and, in fact, is joined, for example, by the people of South Asia, we might actually see an emergence of Asia, an Asia which is neither an area of Western dominance nor merely a concept, a part of the Western repertoire of concepts 'as dominance'.

Friedrich Dürrenmatt, the Swiss playwright, once made a distinction between the great power (*grosse macht*) and a small state (*klein staat*). His distinction was in terms of theatre and literature; he had no 'political' differences in mind. His argument referred to the unfamiliarity and, therefore, unacceptability of cultural and historical references emanating from the small state and, similarly, the almost universal knowledge and therefore acceptability of references emanating from the great power. These words are not Dürrenmatt's but they sum up fairly accurately the point he was trying to make. Some of our writers, especially the modern writers, face a similar reality. This is perhaps truer in theatre than in any other area. In one sense, I suppose, the difference Dürrenmatt talked of was political, after all. I can relate to *Cat on a Hot Tin Roof* much more easily than the Western (or Chinese, for that matter) audience can relate to a play like *Raaste*. Imperialism or colonialism has made us internalize the Western predicament resulting from post-Enlightenment modernity. The process of establishing cultural relationships of understanding in the opposite direction has not happened. This is not to say that the West does not understand the East. It does but in an 'Orientalist' sense or in an archaeologist's or enthnographist's sense. The East is exotic, colourful, energetic (in its art forms, that is), ethnic, mysterious and so on. The modern Indian has accepted this version of India and Asia. The Western view is that modernity is both Western and universal. The currently dominant Eastern/Indian view seems to be that these categories of modernity do not apply to 'us'. We have 'Indian' theatre. Our 'modern' writer's problem is to recreate this 'Indianness'. It now becomes easy to see how the matter is indeed political; for the acceptance, partial acceptance or rejection of universalist modernity involves political choices and political acts.

The modern Indian painter has, on the face of it, solved the problem for himself. Not only does he know the Western tradition very well, he does not necessarily have to carry the burden of ethnicity. His psychology might be Indian but his logic is impeccably modern. For some reason, the playwrights are still not permitted this. Tendulkar is lost in the dazzle of *Ghashiram Kotwal.* A playwright like the present writer would not even figure in a list of major Indian playwrights not only because there could be a genuine question or two raised about his writing, but also because his writing has very little 'ethnic' quality; it has nothing 'folk' about it. His is a didactic play of modern-day Indian politics. What does one make of that kind of writing? Practically every critic seems to believe that a Bond or a Mercer is all right for Britain. They are not all right for Maharashtra or Kerala. Which is why we have to create an 'Indian' theatre. That is where the politics comes in, the politics of modernity versus nationalism, almost. One must say 'almost' because what is true at the level of criticism or a public policy on culture is not necessarily true at the level of enjoyment of theatre. In a city like Pune or Mumbai or Calcutta, the theatregoer watches (good or bad) modern theatre for the simple reason that it relates to his existence in a real (or unreal) way. This kind of theatre may be bad, which quite often it is, but it is not the kind of theatre our national discourse on the subject wishes to celebrate.

We need to look at this national discourse. As a playwright, I have often wondered why the novelist is not burdened with its weight. The modern Indian novelist can be modernist, 'avant-gardist' or post-modernist, if he so likes. A playwright cannot. At least, he is not encouraged to be so. He must instead go back to the epics, to folk tales and what have you. Of course, one can write a good play based on either. I do not have to tire the readers with already familiar examples. The argument, however, is about a play which seeks to discuss modern society and modern politics. That play is not quite frowned upon but it is usually ignored.

In March 1999, Bhaskar Chandavarkar celebrated Girish Karnad (on account of Karnad's becoming the seventh Kannada writer to claim the Jnanpith) as a playwright in the tradition of

Bhasa, Kalidasa and Bhavabhuti. The Pune papers reported his views and Chandavarkar confirmed the fact to me. It is not an argument easy to follow. The three Sanskrit playwrights do not belong to one tradition; between them, they span several centuries. It is true that they drew their material from the epics and Karnad does the same. But such a comparison is indeed tenuous and, in a way, turns Karnad into an icon, an icon of Indian nationalism as much as the each of the three Sanskrit playwrights happens to be. It is not my argument that Karnad should not or cannot be such an icon but that Chandavarkar, or another modernist for that matter, should not be looking for an icon when the need of the hour is that of a canon. This preference for icon over canon involves (historical) inaccuracy and is unjust and unfair to Karnad or anybody like him. No great novelist of India would be, for example, compared to Bana or even Dickens. Why then is this burden placed on the playwright's shoulders? V. S. Naipaul, who does not find much of Indian writing (how much of it he has actually read, I wonder) worthwhile, does mention Premchand as a significant writer.

A civilization-state with more than fifteen literary traditions, each one of them close to a thousand years old, should have made critics more modest. But the colonialism which persists in our postcolonial times prevents us from seeing that the Indian languages are not *grosse macht* (great powers) and that nobody has the time or the need to relate to the experiential or the ideational worlds of these languages. You will not find any modern literature worthwhile if you do not relate to the worlds generated by those works. The fact that most such commentators talk on Indian literatures with pathetically minimal and insignificant familiarity (with about ten works in one or two languages, at best) is demonstrative of the fact that 'postcolonial' consciousness in the postcolonial world has remained colonial. It may therefore be totally wrong and, indeed, misleading to speak of postcolonial literature/theatre.

In that sense, Frederic Jameson's notion of 'Third World Literature' can still be useful. It would then suggest a literature which has so internalized 'the rhetoric of the other' that no dialectical relationship with the other is any longer possible. The First World remains a distant, unrelated reality, with the Third World not even a distant cousin! This is certainly true of several of our playwrights. There was a time when the playwrights were free of that rhetoric but they are now increasingly becoming its victims. Our modernity has to be our own. But that does not mean that our modernity has to reject the world of ideas generated by post-Enlightenment Europe. We do not have to. Nor can we in reality actually do so. It is like rejecting science, perhaps worse.

Not having perceived this, we land up in a situation where, if we need (in theatre terms) anything modern, we turn almost instinctively to European plays. The tragedy is that no matter what the dominant discourse on theatre might argue, we need a modern theatre. We need *our* modern theatre.

It would appear that a curious package has been popularized in our country which consists of the following:

Sanskrit theatre: maybe for practice.
European theatre: for exercises in modernity.
Indian theatre: ethnic excellence and folk.

This neat division (admittedly somewhat simplified) states the problem of a modern Indian playwright. He is being denied his rightful place in the theatre scene. Although 'art' or 'parallel' cinema has helped in popularizing the contribution of some playwrights, it is both distressing and encouraging that their reputations have spread because of their association with that medium. Encouraging, because the reputations of theatre-people have benefited. Distressing, because some people discovered Tendulkar only through his work for the cinema. Almost all obituaries of Utpal Dutt in the Marathi press talked more of his cinema than his theatre. Needless to add, this would reflect upon those for whom theatre shines in the glory and glamour of cinema and not on the playwrights or the theatre people concerned.

This is made worse by the nationalist discourse. We need 'Indian theatre'—one has heard this slogan time and again. Why?

The counterquestion encounters a standard answer—'Because we are Indians. Our theatre must have a distinct Indian quality'. The difficulty with this position is that it involves circular logic. Worse, nothing could be more vacuous. The so-called 'Indian' quality refers to an Orientalist view of India. Indian would then mean how the non-Indian or the Western spectator identifies India. To start with, this tendency was dominant in music. Take for example the term 'ethno-music' (read Indian, Chinese, etc.) which is an entirely anthropological view of culture. There would be nothing fundamentally wrong with it if we considered Beethoven or Bach as 'ethno-music' too. Yehudi Menuhin once complimented Ravi Shankar as being a modern-day Mozart. Ravi Shankar modestly denied himself the compliment by calling Mozart God and asserting that he could never be God! Without meaning to do so, Ravi Shankar placed Indian music among the human activities and European music among the divine. In theatre, something similar is happening. The divine in Indian theatre is either ancient or primitive in the anthropological or ethnographic sense. Modern playwriting in Indian languages would be not only not divine, it would be almost demonic! Very often, the rhetoric of 'Indian' theatre ends up being a polemic against modern Indian theatre as well as against the modern Indian 'word'. I once heard an intervention in a Sahitya Akademi seminar in Delhi about the primacy of the word in theatre being a 'Western' business. Indian theatre was and should be different! There is a figure of speech, *arthantaranyasa*, in Sanskrit. Kalidasa is supposed to be the master of that. All this would have to be forgotten for the primacy of the word (and the *arthantaranyasa* or any figure of speech for that matter) is a Western idea.

The rhetoric of 'Indian' is thus a rhetoric not of being Indian but rather, of opposition to modernity and its alleged universalism. These people would have no problem doing a Shakespeare or an Ibsen. But they would make a modern Indian playwright, whose play explores the predicament of 'Indian' modernity, run from group to group to have it produced. Delhi's record of adaptations of Western plays and its relative lack of enthusiasm for modernist Indian writing would prove the case.

A part of the problem is the canon. Newly decolonized India has always looked for the icon and rarely for the canon. Tagore's plays had to wait for a Sombhu Mitra and Prasad had to wait for B. V. Karanth. Here, no comparison is intended between the two playwrights. But a comparison between the roles of the two directors certainly is. Such long waits are unnecessary in the West. Modernity has made it aware of history. This awareness creates the canon.

In a very specific sense, therefore, having a canon, developing a canon, is a political act. It defines tradition in a modernist way. It would also finally give us an idea of Theatre-India; Theatre-India defined in terms of its canon. Only the modernists can do it. It must be said that they are not being given their due.

Another aspect of this 'being Indian' is the fact that you cannot belong to the whole of India without belonging to a specific part of it. S. V. Ketkar (*jnanakoshkar*), a major thinker and novelist of the early decades of this century, once declared that one cannot be Indian without being a Maharashtrian, Kannadiga, Bangali, etc. There is no other way of belonging to India. A truer word was not spoken. The tendency these days is to impose a sanitized, uniform Indianness on everyone. A devout Hindu sent me a New Year card on 18 March (New Year's Day according to the Indian lunar calendar) which mentioned Vikram Samvat and the *Yugabda* year. But it did not refer to the *Satavahana Saka*. This Hindu organization had clearly forgotten that the Andhras, the Kannadigas and the Maharashtrians follow that method of reckoning the year. Close to ten crore Hindus and their practices were not important in the eyes of this 'Hindu' organization. This kind of error or shall we say cultural blindness is rampant in contemporary India.

Monolithic descriptions, monolithic views. Luckily such practices are not there in Europe which is why it is possible to speak of French or German or English theatre without bothering about European theatre. European theatre takes care of itself, in a manner of speaking. In fact, that is the reason why European ideas have survived and continue to survive.

There is enough analysis of Aristotle there, in fact more so than there is of the *Natyashastra* here. That, however, does not lead anyone to think of turning his writing into a 'sacred text'. It is a text as any other text and it follows that you have to look for sub-texts and, at times, counter-texts, all of which contribute towards enriching the original. We have not done that with our traditions. How many sensible histories of Bangla or Marathi or Kannada theatre are available today for 'national' consumption and 'national' debate? What, then, are we talking about when we speak of a national theatre?

When we speak of a national theatre we do so with almost no knowledge of the various Indian theatres. Part of the reason for this ignorance could very well be the attitude or tendency to treat these concrete theatre traditions as 'regional' or *pradesik* as against an *abstraction* of a national or Indian theatre. It must be emphasized that this polarity is neither realistic nor useful in terms of our theatres. It is important to see that India's tryst with modernity takes different (necessarily comparable) forms in different languages. It is essential for our self-understanding that the unity of Indian cultural expression is achieved through the plurality of linguistic (in this case, theatrical) expressions. For that reason, the terminology of 'regional' is misleading when it comes to cultural production. Each mode is uniquely important. Each one is uniquely Indian. In that sense, there is no regional theatre in India but several equally valid and legitimate Indian theatres.

Once we understand this it will not be difficult to understand that even this plural (i.e. Indian theatres) is no longer necessary; Bangla or Kannada or Marathi theatre would be good enough—each one of them is authentically Indian. The difficulty is that we know very little of them. It is not their regionality but rather our ignorance arising out of our tendency of dismissing them as *pradesik* which keeps us so far removed from the multifaceted and multilingual cultural expression of our people. It then follows that we cannot and indeed do not discuss 'modern' Indian theatre(s). Theatre discussion in our media and elite exchanges also gets divided into three stages, very much like the theatre and its threefold division as pointed out earlier. These three stages are:

Sanskrit theatre.
Folk theatre, martial arts, traditional theatre, etc.
Modern Western theatre.

This approach dismisses nearly two hundred years of modern proscenium theatre in India. It rules out contemporary experience and, therefore, contemporary sensibility. All this has a political meaning. Quite often unintended, but the impact is unavoidable. Modern Indian theatre is a victim of a particular kind of politics—the politics of cultural nationalism which is monolithic, blind and anti-creative.

In any decolonizing and decolonized society, a degree of cultural nationalism is inevitable. Questions of identity and of tradition cannot be wished away or forgotten. At the same time it is true that the discourse of cultural nationalism is, more often than not, grievously flawed. It defines cultural nationalism in terms which are static, dated and often imposed on us by the very people who colonized us in the first instance and who were and are interested in keeping us away from modernity, except in terms of technique and technology. And they have nearly succeeded in their project and now, have, extended that strategy to the arts. They did not and do not want the scientific spirit and universalism to come to the formerly colonized people.

I would be wary of a conspiracy-theory view of the cultural phenomena. I do not intend this. What I argue is that, both in terms of social sciences and the arts, we have set a certain premium on avoiding the questions of modern life. Our folk or traditional art forms were not intended either to analyse or to perceive, in clear terms, the modern problems of modern life. Avoiding them is tantamount to adopting a political position. A neat description of that politics would be giving up one's historical responsibility. And even if you forget the historical responsibility for a while, there is still the question: for who am I doing/writing my theatre? In today's India, urban theatre audiences comprise a phenomenal number. They are also made up almost exclusively of the middle and upper middle classes. They have questions confronting them. Is it not incumbent upon at least some of us to try and tackle them? A Tamasha and a Pandavani are enjoyable. But if they are, we owe it to those forms that the traditional artists practise them and those doing them survive. We as a people seem to have developed a callous attitude which has made an extraordinary situation possible. Modern theatre artists adopt those forms and techniques and perform abroad while the traditional practitioners of these forms have nowhere to go. The story of the Maharashtra Tamasha Parishad is a case in point. This Parishad was founded to help the traditional artists survive. It has failed because the new politics of cultural nationalism does not have the traditional artist in its reckoning. It wants the new high-cash/high-class artist to take over those activities. In the process, a new semantics developed. What was once a Tamasha became Sanskritized *lokanatya*. These semantic changes mark the very antithesis of what undistorted cultural nationalism should be. Worse than that, this semantics suggested a cruel appropriation which involved the virtual elimination of the traditional artist has happened hand in hand with the packaging of Indian art forms for the Western markets. That all this happens in the name of cultural nationalism is amazing indeed.

There is a similar situation staring the modern playwright in the face. History is on his side. Politics is not. What makes it worse is the fact that the languages in which he chooses to write have also been targeted and are on the defensive. The politics of cultural nationalism dictates these things. That politics consists in the packaging of Indian culture for Western markets. There the sensibility and the problems of *kleine stadt* (small states) are scarcely useful. It is not useful just to have history on your side. You ought to have markets and their politics as well.

An Affair to Remember

How does or should one describe one's relationship with theatre? Not a very easy question to answer. There can be both highly personalized, almost autobiographical as well as generalized answers to this question. They, however, need not be exclusive; there will be some autobiography in all such efforts. Since the Enlightenment, we have all tended to look at the arts as social and historical phenomena. The 'personal' has always tended to be a little secondary to the social and philosophical which is probably the reason why 'aesthetics' has dominated Western thought. Anyway, it is not easy to write on the subject I have been asked to handle and, indeed, how does anyone write on this relationship with theatre?

The difficulty arises primarily because, for me, it is a highly personal relationship; a bit like an affair, I reckon. How should one describe an affair? As an immensely joyous relationship? Perhaps yes. But there is no getting away from its illegitimacy. The moment you have written a play, you realize that the pleasure you derived from it was illegitimate inasmuch as it does not really belong to you. The script is somebody else's. It always is. Normally the *karta* (the maker) is different from the *bhokta* (the consumer). In this extraordinary business of theatre, the distinction simply disappears beyond a certain point; the world stands on its head. That is also true in yet another sense. Theatre gives you a bottom-side view of reality; the metaphysical tree of *ashwattha*—a tree with its branches below and roots up in the sky.

All such descriptions do not take away the tormenting relationship that theatre imposes on you. The metaphor of an affair was not frivolous. It was also not intended to answer a question by simply dissolving it. Yes, the question is, in the last analysis, one of morality. Theatre being an autonomous world, it would have not only its own laws but also its own morality. Theatre, perhaps all of the performing arts, teaches you this autonomy, its own laws and its own morality. It is a grand learning experience. What you learn from life goes into theatre and theatre brings it back to you with its own lessons. In the process, life starts looking quite different, certainly very different from when it entered your script. One has often had to answer the question about whether theatre changes life or society or something like that. I have always been at a loss as to the answer. Times without number, I have tackled it thus: 'Look, I don't know all that. But it has certainly changed me'. That part of the answer is still easy. What is difficult is its supplementary (to use parliamentary language) which usually is: 'In what way?' Then I am at an even greater loss. Almost irritably, I say, 'Look, I know it has changed me. I don't know in what way. Just that it has. I may not be a better man but I certainly am a different man.' Writing a script puts places you in a relationship with life which you do not necessarily comprehend. It is not a cognitive experience in the same sense in which the writing of a thesis is. It is not as though it is any the less valid for it. I do not like the category of science fiction precisely because it seems to counterpose science and fiction. The use of the word 'theatrical' is, likewise, problematic. It seems to deny all claims to truth that theatre may make. The truth is, on the face of it, all about certainty. Many years in theatre and you realize that truth has just as much to do with uncertainty.

But then, this uncertainty may and, indeed, does have as much to do with internal, theatrical uncertainty as external worldly truth. You do not realize that the meaning of a word or a pause or a silence can be more or less meaningful than you as an author had intended it to be. Sometimes, it may simply acquire a meaning which was never intended during the writing process; your own text appears almost unfamiliar to you. In an affair, you are never certain if your friend and partner is, in fact, in love with you. An affair must be, in the last analysis, a painful thing, I imagine, precisely because of this uncertainty. So is theatre. It is uncertain, it is illegitimate, it is painful. It is also so different—different every time I witness yet another production of my script. I visit each new production wondering which region of the unknown I am about to enter. I have known playwright friends who do not watch performances of their own scripts and I have often wondered why not. I get the feeling that their sense of *mamatva* (sense of 'mineness', if such a term may be coined) for their writing is quite intense or that they have rather strong views on the meanings that the directors and the actors create from their texts. It is a genuine problem. Like hiding something or, more accurately, not owning a world of experience. It is also denying yourself a world of meaning, or perhaps worlds of meaning.

2

I recall watching three productions of Badal Sircar's *Evam Indrajit.* I must mention particularly the productions by Satyadev Dubey and Shyamanand Jalan. The text used was the same. But the play appeared to be entirely different. In Dubey's production, Indrajit was at the centre of the play. In Jalan's, the emphasis shifted. Both were exciting productions; both were markedly different from each other, almost in contradiction. In the end, Sircar was no longer at the centre of things. His script and the two directors were. In our tradition, the playtext has been described as *ananta-patha* (having multiple readings). My first experience of the quality of multiple significations of a theatre-text was watching these productions.

The text is a powerful force. So powerful that it does not quite recognize either the authorship or the conceptual world of the author. I realized this force in a peculiar way. My play *Andhar Yatra* was being done in Mumbai. One day, I got a near-frantic phone call about Suneela Pradhan, a brilliant actress playing the protagonist of my play, having great difficulties memorizing her lines from the fourth scene. I found that quite strange and said, 'This must mean that either my language has lost its natural rhythm in that particular scene or that Vasundhara (the name of the protagonist Suneela was playing) is saying something she should not be saying'. I reworked the scene over the next two days but, already, Suneela's recalcitrant memory and my text had entered into an alliance and seemed to triumph over the auctorial abilities of one Shree G. P. Deshpande! Vasundhara did speak a different language. Oh god! These texts and the jealous use of their force and autonomy!

Those who are familiar with that text would remember the fourth scene I am referring to. When the young radical is killed in a police encounter, the discussion between Vasundhara and his mentor, also her lover, centres on whether he is now morally bound to join the struggle himself. In the first draft, she had tried to persuade him against this leap into the darkness of more than probable death. Clearly, that was something out of character for her as she had developed until then. The more natural thing for her would have been not to escape the larger moral question. In a sense, the text had already decided which way, she would vote. She could not have persuaded him to opt for a course of action amounting to 'bad faith'. My own text taught me a thing or two about how my protagonist should and would speak and changed her language. Almost as though a miracle, Suneela memorized the new lines with a speed that spoke of Vasundhara's sense of liberation from the unnatural words and position of bad faith. I might add here that the texts are also clever! In this case, it certainly was. It used Suneela's grand memory failure to help me see which way it wished to go. Well, nearly so. The text is both *anantapatha* and *anantapathaka* (multiple reader), one might say.

This kind of experience has convinced me that the dramatic word is twice-born (*dwija*) like the three upper *varnas* of the Indian *varna* system. The word is first born when the playwright writes it. It gets its second birth when it is spoken on the stage. Traditional Hindu logic rates this second birth as higher or more important. You become what you are with the *samskara* that brings about the second birth! The director and the actors are doing that to a playwright's words as they bring them to life on stage.

This is not to say that the second birth of the word is necessarily and always an improved avatar of the word. Sometimes, the second version can simply be a distortion. I do not mean to valorize the played word for its own sake. Nor do I want to suggest that the two births I am talking about be widely separated from each other. As in the Hindu social system, the twice-born is the same individual. It is the business of those responsible for the played word that the 'individual'—common to both written and played word—is not split or destroyed. I have had a few distressing experiences of the ideological world of my word being distorted, if not altogether destroyed. I imagine that there is always a tension between the playwright and anyone or any group who wishes to give the second birth to his word. Most of the time that tension can be a big creative boost to the production. But equally, though not as often as one might fear, it can contribute to the distortion/destruction of the play. It is possible that my friends who do not watch the productions of their scripts are apprehensive precisely of such accidents of history.

3

I will now move away a littlefrom the production of plays and what it can do to the text and speak instead of an extraordinary dialogue that a playtext can and did generate. I refer to an English translation of Kalidasa's famous play, *Malavikagnimitram*. Tawny did an English translation of this Sanskrit classic early in the twentieth century. Tawny was no admirer of John Stuart Mill or so it would appear. Looking at the power of the emancipated Iravati, the queen of Agnimitra, Tawny thought that Mill's position on women's rights and liberty was redundant. And strangely, Tawny introduces an argument in parenthesis against Mill in his translation! An ancient Indian classic being used to settle scores in a (translator's) contemporary debate! The importance of Tawny's strange position lies in the fact that Kalidasa was for him, in a sense, a contemporary. At any rate, he used an ancient Indian play to decide a question on which the playwright had no stated view. Or, simply put, it was a question of which the poor playwright could have made little sense. In short, this was also a case of multiple readings of a play.

Or, think of the following. Tendulkar's play *Ghashiram Kotwal* is easily the most celebrated theatre spectacle of post-Independence India. It is a story of the decadent ruling class of the eighteenth-century Pune court. If you ask yourself what decadence the play is talking about you will realize that it is the sexual mores of the rulers that the play talks about. There must have been, for example, financial corruption. Nana Phadnavis, the powerful minister of the Peshwas of Pune, was called Navakot Narayan (a billionaire). Where did this wealth come from? The playwright is not interested in the problem or so it would appear. In spite of the fact that the play did shock its Marathi audiences when it was first staged, it would be true to say that there has been no other example of such a pleasant and, in a way, harmless attack on the ruling classes. This is not to say that the sexual mores of the eighteenth-century Pune rulers were not decadent. They surely were. But to watch their dramatization a good two centuries after the event can be, and indeed was, a pleasurable experience. A more all-round attack would have established its contemporary meanings. In a briefest possible introductory note, Tendulkar calls it a 'historical fable'. Fables are enjoyable, immensely so, but rarely disturbing.

This is a case of the text and the author combining to create a given kind of impact. Small wonder that this play did not generate anger outside Maharashtra. Within Maharashtra, especially in Pune, it generated hostility largely over the nationality and caste question. (It was taken as an attack on the Pune brahmans and the Maharashtrian ruling class.) It was fascinating to watch two radically different reactions to the same play. Outside Maharashtra it was the grandest kind of theatre. Within Maharashtra, at least of the early seventies of the last century, it was for many almost a betrayal. Tendulkar remains the most famous and one of the greatest playwrights of Maharashtra and is accepted as such in India and abroad. Within Maharashtra, however, he is not exactly anybody's idea of a people's loved playwright. All this, of course, is besides the point. The point I am making is about the different meanings that theatre generates. At times it picks up the meanings which are floating in society and plays with them. It usually manages to have the last laugh. Like *Ghashiram* did. Angry Maharashtrian brahmans rejected it, or appeared to reject it to start with, in the early seventies. Now the written and played words together have brought them round to enjoy it, if not to love it. There cannot be a better example of a play playing with its adversary and turning it into a friend.

Max Reinhardt once said that his birthplace as an artist was the top gallery of the Burg theatre. A neat description of what theatre does to you. One should perhaps add that this is true not only of an artist. I would like to say that it is true also of the modern individual. He is born in a theatre. I certainly was.

The Text and the Play

Chairman and friends! It is a singular honour to be asked to speak at a series of lectures of this kind where stalwarts like Utpal Dutt and Habib Tanvir have spoken. I am aware that I don't quite belong to that galaxy. I do not deserve to. However it was difficult to say no to this kind invitation, however presumptuous it might seem, for one very personal reason. When Rajinder Nath was the Director of the Shri Ram Centre, I happened to be a member of its governing body. It was then that we thought of this lecture series. In fact, I might claim some credit for it. This is the reason why you might notice that Utpal Dutt's lectures carry a preface by me. It was, of course, no more than a coincidence. But then life is made up of coincidences, as is theatre. In a given show you suddenly discover that the usual piece of property is missing. As a performer you have to improvise. The text undergoes a change. Then you go on improvising and the text goes away or changes. The play has to go on. My introduction to Utpal Dutt's lecture is in a sense a wrong piece of property! So it is now. Last time I wrote the preface. Now I venture to write the lecture! I am not tall enough to be here. But here I am.

This question of text and performance has been bothering me for quite some time. I have made a formulation of a kind on the subject. But while stating that formulation I will move forward and backward. I will venture a bit into *Advaitavedanta,* a bit into Bhakti poetry, a bit at folk and the written word, modernity and all the rest of it. Whether a coherent and meaningful argument will emerge at the end of it all, I really cannot say. I hope it does. One argument, it will appear, has been split into three. Therefore, if it occasionally tends to be too academic and too theoretical, you will have to forgive me. I am reminded of a very famous statement by an American director who once said that theatre-people are generally tired of theory—the English find it boring and in America it is virtually non-existent. So, it is that sort of situation. It might appear to you too theoretical. There is a personal reason for that too. Professionally, as a university teacher, I deal in words. My standing, such as it is, is word-oriented.

The text and the play. An age-old question. There have been age-old answers too. Why, then, this re-posing of the question? Age-old questions need to be re-asked. We live in post-modernist times hence some deconstruction of words is inevitable. There is a famous quarrel in ancient Indian grammar (do not be frightened by the word 'grammar'; it has a bearing on the text and the play): What is it that generates meaning? Is it the word which gives meaning to the sentence or is it the sentence which gives meaning to the word? If you take the latter position, you would come close to the dramatic because in drama a word, unless situated in some manner, does not acquire a meaning. So, one of the ancient Indian thinkers on language, Yaska, argued that the meaning of a word can be obtained only partially through etymology. The process of meaning-generation is completed only when the word is related to *prakarana* (which may be taken to mean context). In other words, it is not enough to say that there is the word or, by extension, the text. You have to situate the text. Of course, this could become a circular argument when read in the context of the sentence and the word. If the sentence makes meaning of the word, then how do you read the sentence in the first instance without making sense of the word?

This is very much like the problem which we have in theatre which was, originally, a problem of grammar.[1] This problem needs to be re-posed. It is also one of repose. What I will do is precisely that. An old question will be allowed to re-pose itself, along with the grammarian's certainty of its answers. But the difficulty is that the moment you re-pose that question, the certainty of the answers disappears. That is what happens all the time even if you were to think of a very word-oriented play. Take, for instance, *Andhar Yatra*.[2] Dialogue, dialogue, dialogue, tiring dialogue, boring dialogue, even. There is a difference between the two. A tiring dialogue gives strength to a play; a boring one could ruin it. But the whole question regarding dialogue, tiring or otherwise, is: how do you place a sentence? I will give you a very short illustration of this. All of you must have seen Tendulkar's *Ghashiram Kotwal.* There is a short scene when Ghashiram meets Nana Phadanavis for the first time. I will purposely give you the Marathi sentence because the way you pose that sentence changes its meaning in Marathi and that cannot somehow be captured in translation. There is political geography involved in that dialogue. When Ghashiram comes out with all that praise for Nana, bordering on the obscene, the sycophantic, it must have struck Nana, a Poona brahman, as 'foreign' and he says, *'uttarekadil dista'* (you appear to be from the north). The whole point is that from a Poona brahman's perspective, somebody who uses so much praise clearly belongs to north Indian *court politics*—he cannot belong here. It is an inference which a Marathi audience will immediately relate to. The word *uttar,* which literally means north, then does not become north per se but signifies north Indian *court politics.* Yaska's position, that the word has to be related to a *prakarana,* that etymology is not enough, would apply here.[3] A set of new questions will emerge out of such a re-positioning. Consider what Gramsci has to say in his review of a certain production:

> There is palpable atmosphere of bestiality in the auditorium. It *emanates* from the laughing faces, from the gleaming eyes, from the short and new bursts of laughter from the audience. And yet, their spectators are not lumps of crude flesh and blood wrapped in skin. They are moved, they are able to be moved. They can feel humanity, they can understand pain. They can take on an expression of seriousness. They can feel their eyes veiled by a deep sadness. And yet, when the curtain rises and the ridiculous caricatures of men and women on the stage put their machine in emotion again, the faces relax into dull-witted gaiety and the atmosphere of bestiality increases and grows heavy. One stupidity follows another, piling up into huge rubbish heaps, gawkily overflowing. Boorishness triumphs absolutely over intelligence, it spreads in the applause and deepens in satisfied tittering. It continues to haunt

our steps in the putrid vapours of the evening, in the fogginess of approaching autumn.

You can see there is an audience involved. We talked of the text, the sentence or the context of the word and, naturally, the actor. We now have Gramsci talking of the audience. This audience has to be modern, necessarily modern. This review was written on 3 October 1917, a little more than a month before the Bolshevik Revolution. You had a tired audience in Italy and, historically speaking, you had a rising audience in Russia indulging in another theatre. The text here is a larger reality. In short, whatever else it might have been, it was not a traditional audience. 'The dull-witted gaiety', 'the bestiality' is the reality of modern life—that is perhaps the first point I would like to make. The question of the text and the play is essentially a temporal question: it is bound by time. It depends upon when you are doing a play or working out a text and where. There are no eternal answers as far as the meaning and its generation are concerned. The text is supreme, the play is supreme, the word is supreme, the actor is supreme, the author is supreme, etc. This talk of eternal supremacy of one or the other and the freedom it is supposed to generate is not valid. *Nirankushah kavayah* (the author is supreme), said ancient tradition. That's scarcely true in modern times if it ever was. We are face to face with the dull-witted gaiety of the modern audience. It is looking at the text and playing out a text and textualizing the play. Therefore, Walter Benjamin says, 'Barbarism comes with every masterpiece in the history of culture.' In modern times there is not only the co-existence of masterpiece and barbarism but of various others as well. The text and the play co-exist. The author and the director co-exist. The actor and the word co-exist. The sentence and the word co-exist. As we have seen, our ancestors seemed to be aware of these series of co-existences which is why Yaskacharya laid down: *na ekapadani birnruyate* (never speak of a word in isolation).[4] I keep going back to ancient tradition precisely because there is such a thing as a subconscious socio-philosophical memory of man which makes us act and react in a particular way. Let me cite an example altogether external to theatre which might prove the point I am trying to make.

India is the only country perhaps where *kavi sammelans* and *mushairas* (public readings of poetry) are still held. In no Western society is poetry related to like this. Poetry is something you read to yourself. It is a very private act, especially in modern bourgeoisie society. I cannot think of a situation in which twenty-five poets are participating in a *kavi sammelan* in London. It is not possible there. But, it is possible here and it speaks of a certain time-frame within which we relate to art. And a certain time-frame within which the Western readers relate to poetry. One wonders why we are in these *kavi sammelan* days and they, in the post-*kavi sammelan* era. All relationships to the text are temporal.

The 'bestiality' and 'gaiety' go together because this gaiety can only be dull-witted. This gaiety is at the cost of my own existence at one level. It is also at the cost of the play, the text, at another because in the act of seeing the play I establish a relationship (defined by time) with the text which is both of friendship and hostility. Both these exist together. There are thus two such relationships of friendship and hostility: one, between the actors on stage who are performing the text and the other, between the actors and the audiences who receive the text, thereby textualizing a performance. Modernity gives you an interplay of dull-witted gaiety and bestiality. Shaw once talked of civilization needing both the classic and the trash. Presumably he was describing modern civilization—at any rate, it is a modern view of civilization. The hostility which co-exists in the relationships is probably because we live in hard times. Modern times are hard times, and post-modern times would be disintegrated times.

However, even in pre-modern times there was the awareness of a certain playfulness inherent in theatre. The crucial thing was *lalitya*, which could be translated as playfulness. In Kalidasa, you see that *lalitya* in good measure—there are numerous instances in his *Malavikagnimitram* where the language has itself become a play. The text is presented as play; the performance is a kind of textualization of the play. There is perhaps no other play and certainly none by Kalidasa where the characters seem to be conscious of 'playing' a role. Even the stage instructions say 'she turns around as if angry'. Other instructions talk of 'as if disappointed'; 'as if sorry', and so on. A lovely verse describes Malavika turning away (*parivartyayantya*) 'as if in anger', thus setting a standard of playful acting (*lalitabhinaya*). It is a case of a character acting and therefore an actress acting! This is playfulness on the stage. Hazari Prasad Dwivedi makes this point in his excellent work on Kalidasa.[5]

Kalidasa is, of course, much celebrated as a playwright. There is that famous verse (of unknown authorship as far as I know):

> *kavyesa natakam ramyam*
> *tatra ramya shakuntala*
> *tatrapi chaturthankah*
> *tatra slokachatusthayah*
>
> Drama is the best among all literary forms/Of them the best is *Shakuntala*/In that the best is the fourth act, /And in it just four verses.

This traditional description loses a great deal on the playfulness of text and performance and argues markedly in favour of the word, missing a point in the process. I think quite often that *Malavika* is the victim of this latter-day insistence on the non-performative word. *Malavika* has a text which plays with performative word. Later scholars, overwhelmed by Kalidasa's *arthantaranyasas* (one of the famous figures of speech or literal speech) preferred the beauty of a (non-performative) word. This must be the reason for *Malavika's* decline! So much for the playfulness, inherent in the texts, constitutive of the texts, if you will. This is by way of introduction.

1

We began this discussion with some categories of Sanskrit grammar. That was important, as we saw, in the context of a certain hermeneutics. The early grammar displayed certain liberating features. One of the well-known things about it was its gender-consciousness. Early Sanskrit did not distinguish between masculine and feminine names. A male by the name of Uchchasravas wants to marry a female of the same name. Non-distinction of this kind must suggest that the grammar reflected the problems of social organization. Being a grammarian meant taking a social position. A text or even a sentence or gender was part of a larger text.

There are two texts by Shankaracharya: one is called *Sarirakabhasya* while the other *bhasya* is a commentary on *Gaudapadakarika.* There is a basic contradiction in both. Of course, it could well be a purposeful contradiction. Because one can be certain that a man like Shankaracharya had academic discipline: after all, he was a teacher and, in those days, teachers had discipline. One does not know why a contradiction was employed. We should perhaps take his *Advaitavedanta* not philosophically but playfully. There is in it a very famous problem which arises from the contradiction between two terms: *drishti-srishtivada* and *srishtidrishtivada* employed in the two texts cited. These two terms represent the schools within which the Vedantins are divided.[6] The problem is whether what you see defines reality (*drishtisrishtivada*) or whether what exists defines your vision (*srishtidrishtivada*).

It is a typical theatre problem. How do I relate to this text? I give a text to director. What happens then? Suppose you take that text to be a *srishti.* Then the director looks at it in a particular way, and the actor looks at it in a particular way. When happens next is the case of *drishtisrishtivada.* The vision or the way the text is looked at ultimately decides its character. And that is why you have different productions of the same play, productions apparently using the same text but so different that they appear to be based on different texts. But is it really the case of *drishtisrishtivada* ? That, after all, it is the *drishti* that determines the *srishti*? Perhaps not quite. The *srishti* also made that *drishti* possible. There is always enough room in a given text to make it so. In other words, there is room to look at the relationship between play and performance with reference to these two traditional views or, shall we say, to the apparent contradiction implicit in the traditional views. We are used to looking at the text and the play as separable and separate categories of analysis. Even in a Shavian an Ibsenite play, which belongs to the text-oriented school, this interchangeability or dialectics of *srishti* and *drishti* exists. These plays demonstrate that it is not easy to establish the primacy of *srishti* or *drishti.* The interrelationship between the text and play I am talking about can be related to the contradiction in Shankaracharya's two *bhasyas,* and the contradiction between the two *vadas.* Vedantins also could not come to terms with them. *Drishti* or *srishti* taking prominence remained an unresolved question. Just as well. We can approach the question of the text and performance in terms of these *vadas*. Some use of tradition without being a traditionalist is called for. Seeing determines the text and the text, in turn, determines the seeing. What, then, is the seeing that we are talking of? There is a dialogue in *Hamlet*. Hamlet is with his mother and his father's ghost appears. His mother does not see the ghost.

> GERTRUDE. To whom do you speak this?
> HAMLET. Do you see nothing?
> GERTRUDE. Nothing at all, yet all that is I see.
>
> *Hamlet*. III. iv. l. 130–31

Srishtidrishtivad is not linked only to Shankaracharya. The two realities that Hamlet and his mother see are specific to their *drishti*. I am not saying that Shakespeare was a Vedantin. I am only trying to say that all creative thinkers have been fascinated by this problem of seeing 'nothing and yet all that is' one sees!

In compositions of both Dnyaneshwar and Eknath, there are long descriptions of what theatre activity is all about. In the first *adhyaya* of Eknath's *Bhagawat*, there is a verse which says, 'The actor puts on the robes of a king, yet he knows that he is not the king.' He is merely acting the king. The theory of distancing that everybody is talking about lately is here neatly formulated and impressively stated! It does not have to come to us via Brecht. Alternatively, this verse in the *Eknathi Bhagawat* is a pre-capitalist statement of the actor's distancing! This needs to be said because even our tradition-lovers turn to the Sanskrit tradition and the *Natyashastra* and rarely, if at all, to the vernacular wisdom on the arts and performance. This is the reason why one returns to Dnyaneshwar and Eknath. From Sanskrit literary-dramatic analysis to western Europe is an inadequate journey. A play cannot be fully understood only in those terms.

Somebody like me who is so adamantly text-oriented is talking about it and all those who talk about performance traditions hardly ever do—a paradox worth nothing, perhaps! That is why I take the opportunity of saying it: India is *Natyashastra* and other Sanskrit texts; modern theatre is western European—I find this position taken by the debate on text and performance in our country quite unacceptable. If you then try and look at this business, two things will come across. Dnyaneshwar says in *Amrtanubhava* that what happens is that *drishya* (the seen) and *drashta* (the viewer) disappears, only the *drishti* (the seeing) remains and yet the truth perhaps of all three remains too; *'sach'* is the word he uses.[7] Then you rediscover the *Hamlet* text; it makes different sense to you. Hamlet's seeing is different from Gertrude's seeing.

There is a lovely sentence in early Marx. He says that in the times that we live in, 'our senses have become our theoreticians'. That is the business of the text and the play. When senses become theoreticians, text becomes a play.

2

We will today resumé from yesterday's concluding statement by Marx. The entire statement reads thus: 'The eye has become a human eye, when its object has become a social, human object produced for man and destined for him. Thus in practice the senses have become direct theoreticians.' Yesterday I also mentioned that dialogue from *Hamlet* about seeing, and seeing nothing. A similar sort of concern appears in *King Lear*:

> LEAR. Your eyes are in a heavy case, your purse in a light,
> yet you see how this world goes.
> GLOUCESTER. I see it fleetingly.
> LEAR. What, art mad? A man may see how this world goes
> with no eyes.
>
> *King Lear*. IV. v. ll. 140–44

In short, very much like *Sarirakabhasya*, the question still is: what determines reality? Lear seems to suggest *drishti* does not determine *srishti*. The question is legitimate. But the Vedanta or the absolute idealism of ancient India posed this problem in exclusively metaphysical terms where reality either did not exist in its material/ sensuous form or was simply *chidvilasa*, the playing off of the eternal truth or eternal spirit.

Now we should move on to the other forms of Indian thought via the Charvakas and the Sankhyas. One is this seeing the 'reality' which is social production, to use Marxist language, wherein senses become direct theoreticians. In Sankhya philosophy there is, in fact, a term called *bhojya*, something which you enjoy, something which you consume and entire upper levels of experience are actually related to something being *bhojya*. There is a *bhokta* (somebody who consumes) and there is a *bhogya*. In a sense, we can take the pair of *bhogya* and *bhokta* to replace the pair of *srishti* and *drishti*. It would become, in this discourse, a pair of *bhojya* and *bhokta* who would be *udasina* (disinterested).[8] You see repeatedly, even in the *Natyashastra*, the employment of categories which belong to or are borrowed from the Sankhya school. This may sound very unusual. But that became the kind of India that was constructed for us by the turn of the nineteenth century. German and British romanticism prevented us from seeing the variety and the plurality of so-called Hindu thought. We are used to plurality in terms of Sufi, Bhakti, classical Hinduism and Buddhism, etc. but we do not make enough allowance for the plurality that existed within each of these. Be that as it may, the Sankhya formulation that *prakriti* being *bhogya* presupposes a *bhokta* could very well be related to the theory of drama. A text has to be *bhogya*, which in turn expects a *bhokta* in its play form.

This brings us to the actors. They turn the text into a play. They create, to use the Sankhya category, the *bhogyaprakriti* from the text. Meyerhold was once asked about the difference between his actors and Western actors (i.e. western European). Meyerhold is believed to have replied that his actors think and think dialectically. That was the difference. This difference would be relevant to what we are talking about. The relationship between the *bhogya* (the *prakriti*) and the *bhokta* (the *purusa*) is dialectical and the actor makes it possible.

The *Natyashastra* is, therefore, an actor's/performer's handbook; it is a book of and for the actor. There is, therefore, a good deal of space devoted to speech. There is a description also of disembodied speech which does not come from the actors on stage but may come from the wings. In a given play it could even come from nowhere, an invisible, mysterious point.

These have been categorized in the *Natyashastra* into different forms. For example, *akashasahit*, which does not actually come from *akasha* (sky) but rather happens to be simply an ethereal speech. or even a conversation which takes place in the wings. But there is another interesting exercise there. Thus, of the two forms of speech described in that book, one is the *aparivaryaka* speech and the other, the *janantaka* speech. What is *aparivaryaka* speech? Let us say there are four characters talking. Character A is talking to Character B and only B hears the speech and the rest of the community does not. When one person is party to the speech and the rest of the characters on stage are not, it is known as *aparivaryaka* speech. Usually a stage instruction to that effect is given.

In *Malavikagnimitram,* you have several *aparivaryaka* speeches. Exactly the opposite is the case in *janantaka* speech. In that case one character is not privy to what is being said but the others on stage are. There is a standard gesture to indicate a given speech is *janantaka*: you put your small finger and your thumb together and raise the other three fingers to constitute what is known as *tripataka hasta* (the hand showing a sign of three). *Tripatakahasta* denotes the *antara* (curtain) for a given character. This sign helps the audience to distinguish the *janantaka* speech from the *aparivaryaka.*

So, already a triangular relationship is established between Character A, Character B and Character C, i.e. the audience. Typically, three units act and interact in a play; they do not in a text. What we discussed yesterday with the use of terms like *drishya, drashta* and *drishti* was precisely this; but all three in this triangular formulation belong to one place. *Drashta* and *drishti* are at one place—the vision, and the one who sees are at one point—and *drasya* is at another. That triangle is the Vedanta triangle.

The non-Vedantic triangle is actually made up of three realities: the audience, a character saying something and a character being prevented from relating to whatever is being done or said. A *tripataka* signifies that and, at the same time, establishes a direct link with the audience. No process of theatre is complete without that link; in a sense, the text becomes a play only when that falls into place.

There is so much of talk of *rasa siddhanta* everywhere that one rarely notices that it is less than useful as an aesthetic theory. What actually is possible to argue is that there is really no *rasa siddhanta* in the sense of an aesthetic doctrine. All that the term rasa probably means is aesthetic experience. When it comes to a theory about aesthetic experience, one has to grant that there were probably several. Bhattanayaka propounded one of them. He probably belonged to the Sankhya school. (It is so merrily accepted that India's contribution to aesthetic theory is *rasa siddhanta*, little realizing that there are various formulations of the rasa theory which would deserve mention.)

The range of debate over the doctrine of rasa is simply forgotten. This is precisely what nineteenth-century romanticism about ancient India did. Problems with traditional theatre or Indian theatre or folk theatre come up because we refuse to see the multiplicity of our traditions and debates. There were people in India who argued that rasa is never produced. The only thing that happens, Bhattanayaka argued, is that rasa, a feeling, is generated in one who is watching the play. Something is being enjoyed by the *bhokta* at the level of *aswada* (enjoyment). The rasa is no cognitive event, no *jnana* (cognition or knowledge) comes out of it. It just happens. As I have mentioned earlier, the Sanskrit word for a character or a role is *paatra*: *paatram tarhi kim? Awsadatopayah* (*paatra* means a character; it also means a vessel, a metal glass. *Paatra* brings you enjoyment. Like a vessel carrying wine, it remains untouched by what it carries. Whenever an actor acts, he has to work on distancing himself from the role because a *paatra* cannot afford to be drunk itself—rasa is not produced as far as the *paatra* is concerned. This suggests dominance of Sankhya thought about acting, about play, about how it happens and the just-mentioned three/four relationships which obtain. It would seem that Bhattanayaka's argument comes very close to it.

What happens, however, is that when we come to modern times and 'our senses become our direct theoreticians', we enter a new phase altogether. To an extent we can argue that the Indian tradition has not theorized about 'modern times'. It would not have. It is a recognition so typical of the modern period, a period which begins with large-scale, i.e. industrial, production. This is the period when *paratmakata* (alienation) and, perhaps for that very reason, Indianness, comes into picture. This alienation phenomenon is very interesting. For it brings us to *paatra* again. Consider what Althusser had to say:

> What will become of this ideological self-recognition? Will it exhaust itself in the dialectic consciousness of self? Will it put this infinite mirror at the centre of action or will it rather place it to one side, find it, lose it, leave it, return to it, expose it from two forces which are external like those wine glasses broken at a distance by the physical resonance. It comes to a sudden end as a heap of splinters on the floor.

What is the *aswadopaya* once it is broken? That is why Gramsci said that it is a dull gaiety and barbarism which coexist. It is the classics and barbarism that coexist. They have to, in this sort of situation because everything in the modern world tends to be grotesque. Modern theatre is, at one level, the theatre of alienation but it is also the theatre of the grotesque. It is the violent, the grotesque, that we are all trying to run away from. When we argue about a 'pure' Indian theatre, classical Indian theatre—as has been argued from the time of the Vedas to, shall we say, G. P. Deshpande's time—we mean a theatre beyond time and therefore beyond alienation, beyond reification, beyond the grotesque. Consider the thirteenth-century Marathi text which talked of light and sound: *amhi bolu prakashache bolu* (we shall always talk of light). This *prakash*, this clarity, gets replaced by, if not utter darkness then transitory light or *Daemerung*, as it is called in German. It is not necessarily the twilight which we associate with the end of the day and beginning of the night. *Daemerung* could be a light at the end of the night as well; the word could be understood both optimistically and pessimistically. We talk of this light in prose, in poetry. Now the mystical is replaced by something mystifying. Even in pre-capitalist times, religious or theological documents were considered poetry because they were trying to do something about the mystery of the world. In their own sort of way, this mystery was being analysed and presented as pure poetry. If you read, for example, the hymn to the *usas* (the dawn) in the *Rigveda*, it would come across as brilliant poetry, pure poetry, because man at that time was trying to come to terms with nature. He was dealing with the mysterious and he could do very little with it except, perhaps, to try and understand it in poetic terms. Modern man, however, is in the midst of mystifying things. A certain amount of mystification is growing around him and his poetry or his theatre is trying to relate to this mystification.

In Oscar Wilde's *The Picture of Dorian Gray*, Sybil Vane says, 'I might mimic a passion I do not feel. I cannot mimic one that burns me like a fire'. In pre-capitalist times one spoke of emotions as fires which burnt one and which burned within one. In modern times, we talk or mimic feelings which simply do not exist, cannot exist. Because the more we are into this kind of society, the more we are removed from reality. Modern theatre is a theatre of the grotesque. The reality, too, has to be grotesque or else we would not be able to recognize it. It is like the reality in a cartoon, the finest of which are those where we can identify the person drawn no matter how grotesque. That is what the actor must attempt to do in modern theatre. There is no such thing as, or at any rate should not be, identifying with the role. Modernity being what it is you simply cannot identify with anything.

Think of the famous line from *King Lear*: 'it splits, it splits, it splits'. Modernity necessarily brings with it the phenomenon of splitting. Modern theatre is something that deals with the split. 'The resonance of breaking wine glasses, splinters around.' That is why having or not a message becomes irrelevant largely because both the existence and non-existence of a message assume a certain clarity and modern life refuses clarity. What are you doing when you are doing a play? You are not playing the text of the play. You are playing the text of the entire modern times. Is your Lear relating to the modern times and if so, how?

The question therefore would be: are you playing with the text with this splitting and disintegration in mind? Does your play/playing playing reflect that at all? What text are you playing with and how are you playing the text? What does modernity do to you? What does alienation do to you? Brecht has been rightly described as a playwright of reification which could be understood to mean: turning a human being into a process of an unidentifiable, nameless, meaningless 'thing'. Things are split. If you think of a typical Brecht situation, you will understand the force of the play and you will vividly see the force of the idea that 'we split, we split, we split' in Brecht's characters. Think of Herr Puntila. He is two people in one. There is a drunken Puntila who is extremely gentle and a sober Puntila, a tyrant in his relationship with his slave Matti. When he is drunk, he is so gentle, so friendly that he actually tends to be generous, promises good things to Matti. But the moment he returns to sobriety, he is a tyrant. Brecht suggests that, in modern society, tyranny goes with sobriety and gentleness is possible only under the condition of drunkenness. Gentleness normally has no place in this society that creates splits.

This is also true of Macheath of *The Threepenny Opera*. Macheath combines several personalities within himself; or splits into several, if you like. He is a bourgeois financier who founds a bank as well as a mafia chief. And if any actor doing Mac the Knife in fails to portray these 'splits', the production will clearly fail. He is himself aware of this split and with a view to rationalizing it, asks a question: Is there any difference at all between the founding of a bank and breaking of it? Early in this century there was a Marathi play which had a peculiar character[9] who asked his servant, 'What present shall I give you? Would you like a diamond ring or, maybe a silk dhoti, or perhaps nothing at the moment?' But this character called Phalgunrao is in a comedy of errors of a kind that compares with *Herr Puntila* for a moment or two, although Phalgunrao was pre-Brechtian in a strictly chronological sense. But then his lines, humorous as they are, have nothing to do with the divided self that Brecht is interested in. This division is a feature of modernity.

Srishti is outside theatre, which should govern your *drishti*; *drishti* of those who watch the play, and who do the play, and who read the play, and so on. Towards the end of *Balcony* by Jean Genet, you see a brothel with the character Erna telling the audience that the play is not over and that, when they go home, the same kind of play is waiting for them! Every home, from Erna's point of view, is a brothel where no human relationships are possible. Does it sum up the modern situation or modern predicament, if you will? Our play with the text must capture it.

This is a good place (as any other) to turn to the relationship between the dead word and the living. All theatre is about words.

You might even say that all modernity begins with consciousness of words as words, words as an autonomous or distinct area of experience. Raymond Williams has said that literature, literally, began from the nineteenth century whcich sounds a bit shocking as it would appear to negate Shakespeare, Kalidasa and Molière as literature. But this statement can be understood in two senses as far as theatre is concerned. In one sense, Shakespeare's texts were, in fact, performing texts. Shakespeare did not mean to write plays as literature. It is our perception of literature which makes them literary. An actor/director can read the text strictly as a performance text. The words appear to come from somewhere else! Or almost so. There is a story of a very enthusiastic Shakespearean actor who decided that his old mother should watch him perform. So she did. Then the son asked her how she liked it. She said, 'Not bad, son! You acted well, but this man who wrote this play seems to be a plagiarizer. Every other sentence I heard here was already known to me.' Or words to that effect. Shakespeare's words were, for her, words belonging to somebody else, anonymous words. This illustrates the performative character of Shakespeare's texts or, to put it differently, the performative text and the (literary) text are quite often seen as two different things. I might quote from Bhavabhuti and mistakenly attribute it to Kalidasa. In all probability the quotation has an importance all of its own. I can, therefore, come to you and say, I am sorry, it was not Bhavabhuti but Kalidasa. Separate the quote from the drama itself. This is possible because Sanskrit plays were essentially performative texts the the best example which is any of Bhasa's plays. They are very small texts but when K. N. Pannikar does a show of a Bhasa play, it goes on for at least two hours. Because the actors go on improvising all the time.

When Williams says that literature arose in the nineteenth century, he perhaps suggests that literature established its autonomous character at that time and we started distinguishing between literature, sculpture, painting. All these came to be accepted as autonomous art forms in the nineteenth century. Different art forms developed their distinct aesthetics. The written word claimed a distinct theory and a distinct aesthetics. This happened with the growth of capitalism. The novel announced this change. There is no significant novel in pre-capitalist times. The whole point is that it is modern industry which made the novel possible and literature as an autonomous art form begins with the novel. Once that happens, theatre or the play changes its character. The category of the dead word comes into existence. In other words, in pre-capitalist times, the dramatic words had the opportunity of life, they were living words. With capitalism, a counter-possibility was created that the word was, in fact, dead. When I write a play, I end up putting together a collection of only dead words, constructed in some kind of a framework, if you will, making up part of some kind of a narrative but dead words all the same.

Drama has to begin with the text precisely for that reason. That is the only magic left to us. Strangely, with high industry the magic factor vanishes, the magic factor which comes with the play, with the text. The play has to begin by trying to enliven the text—the text of dead words which are only potentially alive. What the playwright does is to give to the director and the actor a bunch of dead words which can attain life in a production. The best and the worst examples of which would be the dialogue in popular Indian cinema (in any language)! Think of a very fine actor who speaks the most ordinary sentence in the most banal situation. Quite often it works because a dead word becomes a living word with, say, someone like Balraj Sahni. I always remember Nilu Phule, who has acted in hundreds of Marathi films, one worse than the other. But the moment that man appears on screen you sit up and take notice. He plays a very conventional and predictable villain and yet the beauty of it is that he plays the most predictable role in the most unpredictable way. After all, what happens when you act in popular cinema? Say, there is a repertoire of seventy-five gestures. The way you play with these seventy-five gestures is what acting is all about; the way you pause or emphasize a sentence, the way you view a word, and so on.

The word for 'grammar' in Sanskrit is *vyakarana*, but the original meaning of *vyakarana* is analysis—a science of grammar and, in a way, of analysis as well. There have been debates and struggles within grammar which had social significance. Words have been at times terrorists or militants, in a manner of speaking. It is a long tradition. I think all this is a part—conscious or otherwise—of our actor's tradition. It helps him to bring a dead word to life. Somebody might say, Panini would have been delighted if he had known that our terrorists believe that 'terrorist' is not the correct word, the correct word is 'militant'. It is *vyakarana*, analysis, *vislesana*, he would have argued. All that is there. Still, some of the militants think they are not Indians! But we'll let that pass.

The dead word and the living word have meaning other than simple acting. That aspect of play is yet to enter our 'theatre'. Every time I write a play it may not be within my power to write living words. A certain amount of pressure builds around me and I am forced to write dead words. If I am forced to write dead words, a situation in which I usually am, writing forces certain dead words upon me. Then the question arises: who makes the dead living and how? Because that which is forced upon the author is also forced upon the actor. That is why, in common parlance or in Hindi film criticism, you might have read or heard that our actors are 'typecast'. Rightly so, because the film world is called the film 'industry' after all. There is a relation between something being industry and something being typed; in other words, rendering everything faceless. Fortunately this has not happened to theatre, although it has happened partially to commercial theatre in Maharashtra and in Bengal. Nevertheless, theatre is not an industry and it is easy to hide the dead-and-living-word contradiction. This operates on three levels: dead text and live plays; dead atmosphere and possibly live theatre; thirdly, a dead end here and there. In fact, it is quite possible that death exists across the stage and into the audience and that is what is imposed upon you. And when dead prevails and dominates, no play is possible. Play can create life and vice versa.

3

There are many things one would like to say in conclusion. Let me begin with remarks on a different genre of writing. Think of the detective novel. Think of Sir Conan Doyle and Agatha Christie. These names are the best for, among other reasons, everyone has read a Sherlock Holmes or a Poirot story. There is an interesting argument about the detective story. That is what I want to begin with. An argument made by Ernst Bloch, the German Marxist. The argument goes like this. The Sherlock Holmes story belongs to the period of early industrialization. The technique of that story centred on the collection of pieces of evidence. These pieces could be located in a room, a piece of metal or something else left out here or there. Holmes collects them and, on the basis of these pieces, inferentially discovers the murderer. By the time you come to Agatha Christie, the typical horror story, says Bloch, has changed its character dramatically. The assumption now is that almost all characters in the given scene are possible murderers. Once you start reading, you suspect that this man, that person, may be the murderer, and so on. The story is deliberately so constructed. As a demonstration of the Bloch argument, I will cite an account which appears in an Agatha Christie novel published in 1941 where Poirot is talking to his friend about this business of detection. He says, 'You probably think that I collect pieces of evidence from here and there and *inferentially* decide who is the murderer. No, that is not what I do. Remember, *motive* is important.' (emphasis added). Bloch does not refer to this story; I do not even know if he had read this particular story and Poirot's explanation therein. But his analysis of the 'new' detective story is the same. He goes on to add that this is what happens from early capitalism to developed capitalism. In underdeveloped capitalism, everybody is a possible murderer and there is no such thing as (necessarily) an honest man trapped in a situation. This system makes everybody a potential murderer. The only relevant question is whether in that particular case you are a murderer or not.

Bloch says that is why the detective novel, particularly of the Agatha Christie variety, became so popular. I reflected on this situation wherein everybody is a potential murderer. What is the point of this detour of the detective novel? It was done because nothing underlines better the grotesque quality that we earlier discussed at some length. This grotesque quality is the function of our time.

When we think of a modern text and the idea of playing with it, we cannot but do so only in reference to the grotesqueness of the time underlined by a Christie novel. The split personality or the two *avataras* of Puntila reflects that grotesquesness but a production of *Puntila* would fail if the director has not thought about the split personality and its relationship with the grotesqueness of the times. Practically all productions of Brecht in India have tended to fail because they do not capture this 'split' personality. It is this splitting that is important. If you take that argument a little further you will see that the question of the text and the play is also a question of the split. In one sense, this question need not arise. A text has to be done. It has to be played. Why the text and the play? My contention is that it is bound to arise because, in a modern situation, this split has become inevitable. We are face to face with more than one text: one is the social text within which the play happens, then come the words and sentences. That is why we returned to ancient Sanskrit grammar. Does the sentence come first or do words come first? You can relate that controversy to the modern playwright's materials.

Consider these two formulations: one, by Kumarilabhatta, which says that a word cannot have a meaning unless it is related to another word and two, an alternative formulation by Prabhakara. I suppose both belong to the seventh century AD. Prabhakara's position is not the exact opposite. Rather, he formulates the problem differently. He is saying the only meaning the word can have is the meaning in association with other words.[10] They were commentators on linguistics and grammar, and not on theatre. But the point is that if you take all this into account, you come back to the centrality of the split. If, for example, a word and an adjoining word are split, how do you create meanings? There is a way of looking at a Beckett play from a Prabhakara perspective or, alternatively, from a Kumarilabhatta perspective. The meaning of the word: how is that generated? Several answers, perhaps.

The third text we have to keep in mind is the actual performance seen as performance. Why is the question of the multiplicity of texts important? It is the 'why' that is important. This question is not posed in a traditional play. Or at any rate it is posed in a substantially different way. The relationship between the text and the play that I am discussing is essentially a function of modernity and modernism. In other words, the *why* of this question is perhaps not as important as the *when*. When did the split between the text and the play as we understand it occur? Or when was the question meaningfully posed? It is only in writings on modernity and modernism that this question can be posed meaningfully. A Tamasha or a Yakshagana text is so open-ended that a play or a performance can eat it up, in a manner of speaking. The two constitute an organic whole. That is not possible in modern texts because the split between the text and play has come to stay. Further, the split between the text and the play gives us not only a modern play but also essentially a proscenium play. Street theatre does not have this problem in the normal sense of the term, street theatre assumes a split too. The difference is that the street play does not actually face the split *within*. It can survive only in the condition of a split *without*. That is to say, when you have two counterpoles fighting for some kind of control or influence, you can do the street play on the side of the Establishment or rebels.

But what happens in a situation where there is no rebel? I think you have got to recognize somewhere that the idea of a rebel taking over the world is rapidly being defeated by a situation where there may not be a rebel except an imaginary one, a nostalgic one. With the disappearance of the rebel, I suspect that street theatre has no longer any future. The conditions which produce street theatre have either disappeared or are rapidly disappearing, even turning themselves into nostalgia which is not the subject of street theatre. The social text has changed, therefore a certain kind of play is not possible.

There is the curious division when we have these problems relating to the modern theatre. To my understanding the only valid theatre is modern theatre. In all these attempts to do a Pandavani here and a Yakshagana there (by modern people and not by traditional performers), we are being driven to the performance end of the split. Now I am talking of the second split, the text as *samhita*, as spoken word, as an analytical word or, if you like, the original word. As we have seen, *vyakarana* originally meant analysis. If you keep the analytical word in mind, it will be clear that all these attempts at either reviving or redoing these folk forms are counterproductive. It is perpetuating the split. It is tantamount to forcing the Indian people, the Asian people, to the performance end of the split, with the European and the transatlantic world retaining the monopoly of ideas. Thus it amounts to legitimizing the Hegelian distinction between symbolic art (Indian) and classical art (Greek). In a sense, we have already internalized the distinction. Many people in Delhi would rather do a European play if they wished to do modern theatre. If anything 'Indian' has to be done, then even the discerning eye seems to be on the snakes or on the drums. The same is true of Sanskrit theatre. Sanskrit is a great language and nobody can fault my love for it. But doing Sanskrit theatre does not make any sense now. Why is Kalidasa played? Little do we realize that our love for him is no small measure due to the romantic (mainly European) reconstruction of India in the nineteenth century. We are the victims of what Said calls 'Orientalism'.

The time has come to question—if not altogether abandon—this Orientalist perspective. This is not to say that ancient writing should be thrown away. The point is that first we have to emerge as 'moderns' in our own right and in our own languages and then negotiate the tradition. It is only through modernity that we can deal with our social text. No play is possible without coming to terms with that modernity. If we do not pay attention to it, we would perpetually condemn ourselves to a bygone epoch.

As I have referred to in an earlier essay, The Suez Canal was opened in 1869. Why the Suez Canal, you might ask. Well, theatrically you know you do require some alienating acts! Maybe you can call it film technique or cinematic technique. So, let us zoom back. The Queen's representative was there. He made a remarkable speech in the course of which he said that the Canal did not connect two continents but two epochs in time. What he meant was that, in his view, because of the Canal, modern Europe was connected to ancient Asia. You remain ancient, we will look after modernity—that was the imperialist message.

In terms of modernity, Beckett is a legitimate playwright; so-and-so Marathi writer cannot be. That is the implication of the argument because, over the past century and more, the situation has changed. That we have so completely internalized this is shown in the way a play is performed. You require, all the time, some reference or the other to pre-modern India especially for our elite and, of course, the Western audience.

Why was *Ghashiram Kotwal* admired in the United States? Because, I think, of the medieval brahmans moving around in turbans and singing. I have done it myself (here in Delhi and not in the US, I must hasten to add), and I know what it means. Let me add here lest I am misunderstood: *Ghashiram* is a great play.

What I emphasize is what has happened to our plays. Our major musicians perform in Ottawa, Berlin, Toronto, etc. and now they are performing in Delhi. Many introductions and programme brochures actually say so. It would be ridiculous to say that Kishori Amonkar is a great performer because she performed in Berlin. This kind of attitude towards performance represents a different kind of social text. The pre-modern and the modern are now being supported by another text: the colonizing and colonized. The dominated and the domineering. I cannot imagine the Philharmonic Orchestra of a European city actually claiming in their programme brochure that they have performed in Delhi, Mumbai, Calcutta or Shanghai, although they might have performed in all these cities.

Historically, we are being thrown at the performative end not by the script or text of the play but by the social text, because the play has already in its structure internalized these attitudes. We seem to be under this extraordinary impression that the performative tradition is being determined 'there', and assigned to us, in a manner of speaking. We have to create texts which will conform to that construct of a tradition. In the process, this text, both in *vyakarana* and performance terms, is not any longer our text. It is their text and our performance—their text and our play. Our actor indulges in totally meaningless gestures, not related to his social text. The traditional actor does not have this problem; he has his Mahabharata. He is not burdened by Brook's version of the same!

Of course our actors have to be trained in the techniques. But it is perhaps not desirable to make them our play because of the social text that the play would presuppose. It is not a question of revivalism and anti-revivalism. That question is irrelevant. I do not even deny that traditional theatre can be fascinating. That is not the issue. The issue is how one places oneself in this debate. We have to decide if the division by which 'they' produce the text and 'we' produce the play is acceptable to us. For accepting that is accepting relative backwardness.

Then there is this other thing: the contradiction between the city and the country. You might say they are related. Yes, they are. Yet one has to think of the problem that most of the traditional non-Sanskrit Indian theatre was not urban, has not been urban for the last few centuries. It is the theatre of the country. Walter Benjamin said in his perceptive comments on 'Vulgarism, mysticism, myth and leisure; at the same time there is something very primordial. There will be a bit of vulgarism, a bit of rugged sense of humour therein, this mysticism. Anything can happen in these plays. A snake can become a man and the whole story would be woven around it!'

Benjamin was, at one stage, analysing what happens to art in the age of mechanical reproduction. An article I did at one stage, was called 'Art in the Age of Utsavical Reproduction'. There was a time when there was this spate of *utsavas* (festivals) and all kinds of performances happening. You could, at the age of ninety-five, dance for seventy minutes without stop. This, in a specifically historicist sense, is 'primitivism'. Hegel described Indian art as a stage before Art (*Vorkunst*). We do not have to accept this view. Ananda Coomaraswamy had polemicized against it in the thirties. What we seem to forget, however, is that the Western view has not changed. From the Western point of view it is 'primitivism'. It is primary energy. Our elite, however, is out to prove Hegel right. It does so because it gives them a world-view which is apparently flattering and yet helps them transcend politics.

Benjamin has a sharp comment to make on journalism. He said that journalism 'isolates what happens from the realm where it could affect the experience of the reader'. Quite often the so-called pure 'Indian' theatre does the same. What you see on stage is outside and is encouraged to be outside the realm where it could affect the spectator's experience. That is not the case with

Ibsen's Nora or Shaw's Candida. It could happen within your house/houses. You want to leave the theatre quite comfortably. The theatrical experience thus helps you transcend the contemporary social text and, of course, politics. One fears at times that our theatre people practise all those beautiful techniques to effect not only the split with the text but also the split with one's own experience.

In modern times the hero has disappeared. Our theatre world, it would seem, simply cannot do without a hero-oriented text. A modern text is essentially a text without a hero and we have probably no techniques to play such a text. In a traditional dramatic text, you could still project a hero as a hero and play it. Modern play techniques have got stuck in our traditional forms which believed, played and projected a hero, whereas in reality there is no hero.

There is a further problem typical to India but rarely observed in Europe or China. A modern Indian play cannot be done everywhere because of the problem of language. But that is not all. Certain playing techniques are perpetuated in this country in a way in which the distance between the modern text and modern play forever increases. There is all around discouragement of the modern play. Get a folk tale. Turn it into a play. By and large put a lot of music into it, and so on. The net result is that ours must be the only country where playing techniques have very little to do with the text. Lots of play with scarcely a text!

In Yakshagana there is the *antara*—two people holding a cloth from one end to the other. Why does a modern character have to hide behind the *antara* as is seen in 'modern' productions? There ought to be some textual reason behind it. But there is none. The reason is that it was always done so. I saw a production of *Shakuntalam* in Mumbai. Every single detail recommended by the *Natyashastra* was there. Why? It is provided in the *Natyashastra* that musicians sit backstage and one actually saw the musicians on stage, something we have not done for the last one hundred years. The first modern play was done in Calcutta in the mid-eighteenth century, an English play directed by a Russian. So modern theatre has a history of close to two hundred and twenty-five years, longer than the history of the United States as we know it. My point is that everybody seems to dismiss two hundred years of the history of modern theatre in India.

You may call it jargon, and jargon it probably is, but we have got to reject this split between the text and the play which makes the text 'their' monopoly and leaves us with the play alone. To the advanced West belongs the text and we, the smaller people, are reduced to the play. This is the most important split. Tradition shall have meaning only in the context of modernity. We are told that there need not be modernity—only tradition. Please do not ignore the quarrels in Sanskrit grammar because they were reflective of the social tensions of that time. Buddhists were taking certain positions. How do you infer? How do you put meaning into the words, into performance? I have nothing against performative tradition. I am only saying that this business of separating the text from the play has gone to such an absurd extent that, in developing countries, the text has completely become a poor man. If you do not believe me, take any institution which does plays here. You will see that almost all modern plays are European plays, Greek plays or plays by Shakespeare or Tennessee Williams. This makes our theatre activists 'travellers without luggage'. This split has to be opposed. The text-play relationship thus is a political question in the final analysis.

Notes

1. The late Prof. G. T. Deshpande's excellent book on Indian science of literature (*Bharatiya Sahityasastra*) discusses at some length the relationship between grammar and poetics and also between grammar and the ideas of Bharata and Abhinavagupta. See especially pp. 49–52. The book, first published in Marathi in 1958, has since been translated into English and Hindi. The page numbers given here refer to the third edition (pub. 1980) of the original Marathi.
2. The reference inevitably is to my play. It has been translated into English as *Passage to Darkness* published in G. P. Deshpande, *Political Plays* (Calcutta, 1998).
3. Yaska's *Nirukta* lays down:

   na tu prthaktvena mantra nirvaktavyaj prakaranasah

> A mantra should not be understood/explained in isolation, but with reference to the *prakaranam*.

This discussion is based on D. L. Adoni's Marathi text 'Bharatiya Arthavicaraci Purvapithika' ('Introduction to Indian Theories of Signification and Meaning'; 1995) in *Bhasa ani Jivan,* VOL. 13, NO. 4, pp. 46–62. On page 49, Adoni argues that Yaskacharya's equal emphasis on *prakarana* and *vyutpatti* (etymology) is in keeping with the centrality of context.

4. Ibid.
5. Hazari Prasad Dwivedi, *Kalidasaki Lalityayojana* (in Hindi) (Delhi, 1970) p. 103. The verse appears in Act IV of the play. The last line of the verse says that in her turning around she has 'taught' us *lalitabhinaya* (*sandarshitaiva lahitabhanayasya siksha*).
6. For Shankaracharya's positions in the *Sarirakabhasya* and his *bhasya* on the *Gaudapadakarika,* see Surendra Dasgupta, *History of Indian Philosophy* (Calcutta, 1975), VOL. 2, pp. 80–81. My discussion is based on the summary of this debate as given in B. R. Joshi '*Drishtisrishtivada*: Sant Dnyaneshwar and Berkeley' (in Marathi) in *Paramarsha,* VOL. 18, NO. 4, February 1997, pp. 19–25. I must also add that my interpretation and use of the terms would raise many legitimate questions. It should be remembered that even this academic is 'playful'.
7. *Amrtanubhava,* 7.204. One must add that the whole of Chapter 7 discusses the question of *drishti, drashta* and reality. This work has been translated in to English by D. P. Chitre and was published by the Sahitya Akademi (Delhi, 1997).
8. The *Sarvadarshanasangraha* by Madhavacharya in its commentary on Sankhyakarika 57 says:

   > *Prakrtirhi bhoghtyataya bhoktaram purusam apekshate.*
   > (*Prakriti* itself being *bhogya* presupposes a *Purusa* who is *bhokta*)

   See *Sarvadarshanasangraha* (Sanskrit original, translated into Marathi and edited by Prof. R. P. Kangle (Mumbai, 1985) p. 368.
9. *Samshayakallol* ('Comedy of Suspicions') by Govind Ballal Deval, in many ways an unparalleled success on the modern Marathi stage.
10. This summary of Kumarila and Prabhakar views is based on Sreepad Bhat's Marathi treatise, *Poorvamimamsadarsanacha Sabdabodhavichara* ('Poorvamimamsa Philosophy on How the Meanings of Words are Generated') in *Paramarsha,* VOL. 11, NO. 4, February 1990, pp. 333–47. The Kumarila-Sabara position is known as *Abhihitanayavada* and the Prabhakara position is known as *Anvitabhidhanavada.*